The **NO-NONSENSE GUIDE** to

DEMOCRACY

NEW UPDATED EDITION

Richard Swift

'I strongly recommend you check
out the *No-Nonsense Guides*'
Howard Zinn

The **NO-NONSENSE GUIDE** to

DEMOCRACY

Richard Swift

'Publishers have created lists of short books that discuss the questions that your average [electoral] candidate will only ever touch if armed with a slogan and a soundbite. Together [such books] hint at a resurgence of the grand educational tradition... Closest to the hot headline issues are *The No-Nonsense Guides*. These target those topics that a large army of voters care about, but that politicos evade. Arguments, figures and documents combine to prove that good journalism is far too important to be left to (most) journalists.'

Boyd Tonkin,
The Independent,
London

To my son, Josh.

About the author
Richard Swift is a former co-editor of **New Internationalist** magazine. He has worked in radio journalism and alternative publishing for many years and is currently freelancing. He has a long-standing interest in questions of ecology and democracy.

Acknowledgements
Special thanks to Larry Gordon, David Wallace, Jeremy Seabrook and especially Jonathan Barker for their invaluable comments on the text.

The **NO-NONSENSE GUIDE** to

DEMOCRACY

Richard Swift

BTL

The No-Nonsense Guide to Democracy, Second Edition

Published in Canada by
New Internationalist™ Publications Ltd. and Between the Lines
401 Richmond Street West, Studio 393   720 Bathurst Street, Suite 404
Toronto, Ontario   Toronto, Ontario
M5V 3A8   M5S 2R4
www.newint.org   **www.btlbooks.com**

First published in the UK by
New Internationalist™ Publications Ltd
55 Rectory Road
Oxford OX4 1BW
New Internationalist is a registered trade mark.

© Richard Swift / New Internationalist 2010

Series editors: Chris Brazier and Troth Wells
Design by New Internationalist Publications Ltd

 Printed on recycled paper by T J International, Cornwall,
UK who hold environmental accreditation ISO 14001.

Library and Archives Canada Cataloguing in Publication

Swift, Richard, 1946-
        The no-nonsense guide to religion / Richard Swift – 2nd ed

(No-nonsense guides)
Includes index.
Co-published by New Internationalist.
ISBN 978-1-897071-63-2

1. Democracy. 2. Democracy–Developing countries. 3. Globalization.
I. Title. II. Series: No-nonsense guides (Toronto, Ont.)
JC423.S937 2010   321.8   C2009-907291-2

Between the Lines gratefully acknowledges assistance for its publishing
activities from the Canada Council for the Arts, the Ontario Arts Council, the
Government of Ontario through the Ontario Book Publishers Tax Credit program
and through the Ontario Book Initiative, and the Government of Canada through
the Book Publishing Industry Development Program.

Foreword

ONE OF THE main themes of *The No-Nonsense Guide to Democracy* is Richard Swift's cogent argument that the free market – contrary to mainstream commonsense – is an anti-democratic force. Under the ideology of the free market, the market 'decides' vital social matters that in a democracy would be decided by the people. And not surprisingly, the free market *always* decides that some will get (stay) rich and others will get (stay) poor. Moreover, as the market image comes to permeate society as a whole, it begins to shape the political world as well, and citizens are transformed into 'consumers of politics', an audience for the antics of political superstars.

Globalization, Swift argues, carries this a step further. Decisions vitally affecting the lives of the people are taken out of the hands of the state (where the people had some chance of influencing them) and raised to the 'political stratosphere' of international trade and finance organizations (where the people had no chance of influencing them – until Seattle).

Globalization reproduces inequality in a different form, and simultaneously protects the privileged against its effects. The 'democratic' propertied class in the capitalist countries of the Global North guard themselves against a 'vote against all property' by 'exporting' the most impoverished section of their working class to the Global South. In this case, decisions that affect the lives of these workers are made in a different country, where under the nation-state system they have no voice – if indeed they have any political voice in their own countries, many of which are military or other forms of dictatorships. Of course this system is as old as colonialism; 'economic development' and 'globalization' are only its most recent incarnations.

Swift makes clear that 'democracy' is not the name of a system of government existing in certain countries, but rather the endpoint in a struggle that has a long way to go. If, as the End-of-Historyians say, with the demise of socialism, democracy is all there is, then fine, let's get down to it. Moreover, for a radical democrat like Swift, this does not mean simply tinkering with institutions or supplementing the list of human rights. A shift away from what he calls the 'strong market/weak democracy model' requires not only a change in institutions, but also a change in ethos, from the ethos of political consumerism to the ethos of citizenship. This possibility is not something that exists only in the realm of abstract theory, but is something that we see, at least in partial form, in daily life. Swift writes of the 'democratic outbreaks' that occur from time to time around the world, where people 'fly to assemblies' (Rousseau) and start taking matters into their own hands. He argues that there is a 'democratic impulse', a natural, commonsense desire to run one's own individual and community affairs, which exists everywhere, and is different from the 'democratic' ideology preached by the West. Democracy understood in this way can form the basis for understanding and solidarity among peoples who live in very different cultures, but who share the democratic impulse.

One of the attractive things about this book is that it is written in democratic prose. So many democratic theorists make their writing inaccessible to the people they claim to be writing for, by writing in what amounts to code, which can only be decoded by a tiny inner circle of people around the world who have received their initiation in certain postgraduate institutions. How can one believe the democratic aspirations of such blatantly élitist writing? Swift's writing is straightforward and honest, with no escaping into unneeded abstraction or showing off with fashionable jargon. He says what he means, no more. That's how democrats should write.

C Douglas Lummis
Author of *Radical Democracy*

CONTENTS

Introduction

Since the first edition of this *No-Nonsense Guide* appeared in 2002, democracy has taken quite a beating – not least from those who set themselves up as its main defenders. Fundamentalists (of all stripes) obviously place their received 'truths' over a mere set of arrangements where the public get to decide what is true and what is not. That they are a continuing threat to democracy is no great surprise. But the response of the political class to this has, with a few notable exceptions, rallied around the garrison state, with its various doctrines of national security, and there has been precious little concern for the freedoms that have been trampled on in the process. We have been confronted by a new and frightening vocabulary – preventive detention, 'black holes', extraordinary rendition, coercive interrogation, weapons of mass destruction, warning systems based on various colors (amber alert), high-value suspects, and illegal combatants. Terms and concepts like these seek to justify arbitrary action by those in power to forestall catastrophe. Democratic rights just seem to get in the way.

One of the goals of this book is to make the case for a dual democracy – one that includes both a negative 'freedom from' and a positive 'freedom to'. In societies organized around the market economy, 'freedom to' has by and large been expelled from political life and lives on only in the dog-eat-dog world of market activity. By these standards, the job of democracy is to provide freedom from interference with the pursuit and enjoyment of property (in our era particularly corporate property). 'Freedom to' in a collective sense (the stuff of strong democracy) is thus in contradiction to freedom from interference in the market. At the end of the first decade of the new millennium the costs of this lack of 'interference' in the market – at minimum, some kind of effective regulation – are all too apparent. In their restless search for profitability, the powerholders of the market have brought the global banking system, housing markets and much else to the brink of collapse. As usual, those who are suffering most are not those who are most responsible. A good time, one would think, to make the case for a more robust democracy of everyday life where people are given a real say over basic economic and political decisions that shape their lives.

But it is the growth of arbitrary police and military power in the open-ended search for 'freedom from terror' that has so alarmed civil libertarians, as hard-won political and legal rights have come under increasing threat. It is tempting, in an era when democratic rights seem so fragile, to circle the wagons in defense of a few core freedoms. This, I think, would be a mistake. For, as this *Guide* argues, 'freedom from' is inextricably connected to 'freedom to'. The alienation that leads to violent protest and terror can in some profound sense be laid at the door of a lack of freedom. The frustrations that well up in refugee camps, urban slums, neglected villages, and so many other places without hope, need both freedom from arbitrary interference and freedom to participate in a robust political culture. Both are essential ingredients of a strong democracy.

Richard Swift
Toronto, November 2009

1 What is democracy?

Recent confrontations over issues such as war and corporate globalization have yielded some interesting juxtapositions over the meaning of democracy.

THE IRONY OF these juxtapositions came home to me a number of years ago amid clouds of teargas during the massive demonstrations against the extension of the current North American Free Trade Agreement (NAFTA) to include all 34 countries of the Americas but excluding Cuba. The Canadian Government had decided to expropriate the center of Quebec City by slapping up a four-kilometer fence, thereby creating a 'no-go' area to protect 'our' leaders from an unruly public. Over 6,000 police were marshaled from across the country to defend the fence against the thousands who gathered to protest the secret negotiations. The proposed Free Trade Zone of the Americas (FTAA) was designed around the notion of open markets and the rights of corporate investors. It assumed a particular model of 'let-the-market-decide' economic development. This model would squeeze out certain political and economic options – everything from a vibrant public sector to controls of speculative capital would in effect be ruled out. It thus significantly narrowed the democratic policy choices available to people throughout the hemisphere.

The conference agenda was a familiar one – deregulation, privatization, downsizing government. In short, the same agenda that eventually plunged us into the 2008/09 credit crunch and financial meltdown. The 'free' in free trade is the tricky part. Free means democratic doesn't it? Not really. In effect our environmental and social rights were being traded away. No matter what we wanted as democratic citizens, corporate-inspired globalization was what we were going to get.

The battle of Quebec raged for three days. Tens of thousands rallied to say no to corporate globalization and put forward the idea that 'other Americas are possible'. The forces of order filled the Old Town with tear gas at a rate peaking at 30 canisters a minute. Many Quebecois couldn't even stay in their own apartments. Hundreds were injured. Hundreds more were arrested, often on the most trivial of pretexts. The high point of the proceedings from an official point of view was the signing of a 'democracy clause' that committed all the leaders to maintaining elected civilian rule. It also achieved the US aim of isolating Cuba from the proceedings.

But this seemed to those of us on the other side of the fence a rather hollow definition of democracy. How could our leaders be meeting in secret to develop a program that would restrict our democratic rights and possibilities and still call it democracy? Did the word mean anything at all?

Is it okay, as the authorities claim, for politicians with democratic credentials (in other words, they were all in some way elected) to behave in an undemocratic manner? Is it the case, as many politicians believe, that once elected they can act as they choose as long as they aren't caught breaking any laws?

Few of the politicians at the Quebec summit had been elected on a mandate of trading away the rights of their citizens. Trade deals are for the most part not debated at election time. Instead, election campaigns mostly involve the usual set of vague commitments to good government and public order. Some, though, would have promised greater social justice, a narrowing of the gap between the rich and the poor and a cleaner environment. Yet here they all were taking actions that would make these promises difficult, if not impossible, to keep. Was this democracy?

On the other side of the fence were the protesters. The corporate media was by and large hostile to this

What is democracy?

'unelected mob'. But in a democracy isn't it the role of citizens to take a vigilant interest in public affairs? When people see their rights stunted and diminished (indeed privatized), isn't it their democratic duty to rally to defend them? It felt like what the conference organizers really wanted was not active citizens at all. What they wanted was consumers of 'good news' who would sit in front of their TV sets and nod enthusiastically at all the limos, photo ops and final communiqués.

We have been treated to other recent examples of our political élite giving us not what we wanted but what they thought we needed. The invasion of Iraq in 2003 was the classic example: even with opinion polls and millions on the street saying 'no', we got eight years and counting of bloody conflict. It just didn't seem to matter what we actually wanted.

The events in Quebec City raised for me some serious questions. Is democracy just about elections and voting every few years for someone who will then tell you what is best for you? Or does it have a wider definition? Is there buried in the history of democracy a more radical model in which citizens rule themselves? If so, how have we managed to get so far away from that? And is it possible to get back?

When the demonstrators in Quebec breached the security fence I saw that as a victory for democracy. Those in power saw it as a violation of democratic law and order – an unwelcome interference with the democratic process. The same drama about the meaning of democracy is being rehearsed nearly every time the global political class meets to make decisions behind closed doors. Whether it is in London or Pittsburgh, people on the street are proving increasingly reluctant to surrender their decision-making power to those who supposedly 'represent' them. Will it ever be possible to bridge the gap between two such dramatically opposed visions of democracy?

2 Democratic malaise

*'The inalienable right to sit on your own
front porch in your pajamas, drinking a can
of beer and shouting out: "Where else is this
possible?"'*

Peter Ustinov on US democracy.

**While democracy has triumphed as the political
system of choice, there are increasing levels of popular
disaffection. Voter turnout and other indicators of
popular participation are in precipitous decline. The
average citizen is feeling estranged from the political
process and the more-or-less permanent political
class that has come to dominate it. Money and
those who control it easily shape the results of
democratic decision-making. This is causing a crisis
in the meaning of democracy.**

IT IS HARD to find anybody these days who doesn't
believe in democracy. This was not always the case. Up
until the mid-1800s, when movements for democratic
rights began to grow in earnest, democracy was
generally held to be a dangerous idea associated
with barbaric mob rule that would likely destroy all
civilized values if it ever caught on. It was only very
reluctantly (and after a hard, often violent struggle)
that those without property were granted the full
rights of citizenship. It was not until well into the
20th century that the franchise was even extended to
women. And it was not until after World War Two
that the colonized peoples of Asia and Africa were
considered 'mature' enough to decide their own fates.

But times have changed. Democracy, or at least its
mechanics, are now the common currency of political
life. It is meticulously studied in academic journals
and university seminars. Journalists and pollsters
build their careers sorting through the tea leaves to

ascertain the underlying attitudes and behavior of both voters and the politicians they elect. Almost all public policy debate is couched in terms of what people want/desire/need. Even dictators invoke a mysterious 'will of the people' to explain themselves. Not since 'the divine right of kings' has there been a significant political theory that was based on criteria in which democracy had no place. It would probably be just about possible to identify two openly anti-democratic strands of contemporary political thinking – religious fundamentalism of several stripes and technocratic authoritarianism. However, in both these cases a significant part of the appeal is based on the notion that people need/desire (if they only imperfectly realize it themselves) the values embodied by a community of believers or the application of rigorous science to public policy.

The Obama factor
'The election of Barack Obama is a vindication of democracy.' In 2008/09 this statement has the status of an almost universally acclaimed truth. Not only does the first black President have high approval ratings among US voters but he is a source of fascination and enthusiasm in such traditionally anti-US places as France and Latin America. Even the 'Arab Street', as journalists describe popular opinion in the Middle East, made positive noises after the November 2008 US elections. Obama t-shirts are on sale from Jakarta to Johannesburg. Who would ever have thought that they would see the day when a black man became President of the US? Like his hero Abraham Lincoln, Obama shows that the journey from log cabin to White House is still possible. And it's not just his underdog roots. Obama is promising a new politics. Hope. Change. An end to partisan bickering. It can't get much better than this. Can it? Well, yes and no. Or maybe no and yes.

The first edition of this *No-Nonsense Guide to Democracy* started off with the story of George W Bush's stolen 2000 election and the sad tale of political manipulation in the state of Florida. The Bush Presidency was further tarnished by the stubborn fact that a majority of voters had gone for another candidate. It was a bad news story for democracy but only with seven years' hindsight do we realize just how bad. Giveaways to the rich, speculative bubbles, runaway debt, economic collapse, and an endless war on terrorism that undermines basic democratic values – all are part of the Bush legacy. During his 2004 re-election campaign Bush's Republican team pulled another series of dirty tricks to disenfranchise poor and non-white voters in the swing state of Ohio.[1] Democracy was reeling.

But in 2008 the Obama campaign injected a badly needed breath of fresh air – new voters got involved, hope drove cynicism to the margins, democratic idealism was on the march once more. In these circumstances it seems querulous to dampen people's spirits with skepticism. There is no doubt that, after the Bush years, Obama stands as a much-needed ray of light. But there is a disturbing vagueness about the substance of the Obama campaign slogan of 'Yes We Can!'. Can what?

In its own way the Obama Presidency is as enlightening a snapshot of the causes of the democratic malaise as was the heavy-handed thuggery of Bush and his neocons. Here we have a President with an almost unprecedented mandate for change in circumstances that cry out for radical solutions. From climate degradation to economic collapse to endless cycles of war – we desperately need something different. Little wonder US citizens and those around the world look to Obama as a savior-like figure to lead us through the dark days ahead. But despite his eloquence and undoubted intelligence, how likely is this?

Obama is limited in what he can do by two factors

that consistently sap the promise of democracy in many countries.

- In government he has come to rely on the same group of insiders who helped to create the current problems.
- Outside his administration, meanwhile, the wealthy and powerful and their representatives have geared up to blunt any radical edge that may survive the insiders' efforts.

In his choice of economic cabinet members and advisers Obama has picked a group of men who are acolytes of former Clinton Treasury Secretary and Citibank board member Robert Rubin. Larry Summers, Jason Furman, Andrew Mellon and Timothy Geithner are, to varying degrees, responsible for exposing US banks to the speculative derivatives market by deregulating, thereby removing the protection that surrounded traditional banking. Obama has now put these men in charge of a public bailout that is delivering billions in public funds to banks such as Citibank to cover their speculative losses.

The other group of economic advisers with the ear of the Obama Administration is grouped around high-tech industry. Google CEO Eric Schmidt is a mainstay of Obama's inner circle and an able advocate for a research and development revolution to underwrite Silicon Valley. In foreign and military affairs, Obama advisers include Hillary Clinton, who has solid credentials for supporting US military intervention around the globe, and George Bush-holdover Robert Gates as Defense Secretary, who has a similar pedigree.[2]

So if the 'change' Obama promises is to occur, it is not likely to be in the areas of greater economic equality or the substance of US imperial policy. The sad fact is that these kinds of key positions are restricted to a couple of thousand potential appointees, whether Republican or Democrat, who differ more in style than in substance. When it comes to the fundamentals of underwriting corporate America or US military hegemony, dissident views are kept on the margins of power. A similar pool of potential appointees can be found in most 'democratic' political cultures anywhere on the globe. Left or Right, the decision-makers and advisers are drawn from a narrow élite constantly recycled depending on the inclinations of the party in power. The 'continuity' and 'stability' they offer is brought at the price of blunting any push for more radical change.

The constraints facing Obama outside of his administration are also quite significant. Obama was elected with the largest majority in recent US political history and enjoys Democratic majorities in both the House and Senate. Yet from the beginning he has had problems bringing in even minor changes, as 'moderate' Democratic Senators such as Kent Conrad of North Dakota and Mary Landrieu of Maryland are balking at removing tax breaks that Bush brought in for the super-rich (those who make more than $250,000 a year). As *New Republic* editor Jonathan Chait makes clear: 'Unless you are a high-school student reading this article in your civics course, in which case I am sorry to dispel your illusions, you will not be stunned to learn that the affluent carry a disproportionate political weight with the élites of both parties. So while people who earn more than $250,000 per year make up a tiny slice of the electorate, they make up a huge chunk of any congressman's friends, acquaintances and fund-raisers.'[3] The top three per cent of income-earners provide over a third of US campaign contributions.

Similarly, efforts to remove billions of dollars in controversial agricultural subsidies that hurt poor farmers in the Global South (and could help provide the economic means to bring in a coherent national health program for poor US citizens) are being blocked by Senators like Conrad and Nebraska's Ben

Nelson (making common cause with Republicans) even though they only apply to agribusinesses that take in more than $500,000 a year. Obama's difficulties in closing the notorious 'extra-legal' US Guantánamo prison complex in Cuba is another case in point. Even one of the most powerful politicians in the world is stuck with a system whose conservative bias and in-built inertia makes significant change difficult.

Examples are not hard to find. Obama's popularity is unlikely to be able to withstand a term of frustrated promises for 'change', particularly against a backdrop of recession fears. Already a know-nothing 'lynch mob' is being mobilized to attack Obama's already watered-down proposals for a national healthcare system in the US – the centerpiece of his program for change. In a situation of political illiteracy, democracy is easily undermined by fantasies of Obama the black communist planning death panels to judge whether ageing US citizens get to live or die. The ingredients are all here for a savior to become just another example of 'politics as usual'. The point is not to deride Obama, who is obviously a politician of intelligence and insight. His pronouncements about the world getting rid of nuclear weapons show real political vision. But despite the media obsession with the personalities and peccadilloes of politicians, these are ultimately not that important. The point is that US democracy (along with most other democratic systems) is sorely blunted as the means of fulfilling the promise of democratic change.

In some times and places – and Salvador Allende's Chile was the classic example for a generation – too great a commitment to democracy runs the risk of brutal military intervention. But most cases are not nearly so clear cut. In other countries the factors limiting democratic change may vary: hostility between different ethnic groups (India, Fiji and many African countries); fear of the military (Thailand, Ethiopia,

Russia); religious fundamentalism (Afghanistan, Iran, United States, Israel); hostility to outsiders such as immigrants (many European countries). These combine with other factors such as political apathy, the abuse of democratic process by entrenched interests, depoliticization through reliance on technocrats and experts, outright corruption and maintaining a cloak of secrecy around governmental affairs. All democratic systems are subject to such influences to some degree.

Democracy triumphant

Yet despite its problems, popular enthusiasm for democracy, particularly where it did not previously exist, remains high. Take the 2009 elections in Indonesia – with 38 political parties competing in simultaneous national, provincial and district elections. In strictly quantitative terms, Indonesian participation must have the country's former military dictator General Suharto rapidly rotating in his grave. Ten years of democracy and the voter abstention rate has only gone up slightly, from 25 per cent to 28 per cent – not bad by the standards of most industrialized countries.

Over the past two decades, it has been dictatorships rather than fragile democracies that have become the falling dominoes of Cold War mythology. Both military dictatorships and communist one-party states have been in dramatic retreat. Whether in the former Soviet republics of Asia or in the 'liberal' communisms of Eastern Europe, autocratic state rule – mired in economic malaise and under intense popular pressure – has folded like a proverbial house of cards. Even the most sinister *bêtes noires* of the Cold War – the Prussian Stalinism of East Germany and the mighty colossus in Moscow backed by the once ferocious Red Army – have been swept away by 'people's power' revolutions. They have been replaced by a series of regimes with claims to at least some kind of political pluralism. In Russia, however, such changes have proved ephemeral, with 'strongman' regimes reasserting themselves. But only the communist states of the Far East and the isolated little island of Cuba remain bastions of one-party communist rule.

In Latin America the military has been forced back to the barracks in country after country, particularly in the Southern Cone, although countries like Venezuela and Colombia still suffer from significant militarization. The latter remains the last major beneficiary of the kind of US military aid and training programs (part of the seemingly endless War on Drugs) that once helped keep most of the continent under the military thumb. In general, the continent has swung solidly to the Left, with an enthusiasm not just for political democracy but for an economic democracy based on greater equality and social justice.

Bolivia (with an indigenous majority) has its first indigenous President, Evo Morales, while Chile's President, Michelle Bachelet, is not only a woman but

Electoral democracies

Many more countries are considered to be electoral democracies than was the case two decades ago – 119 of 193 countries (62%) in 2008 compared with 76 of 165 countries (46%) in 1990. But the difference is less marked when it comes to showing the percentage of world population living under democratic rule, as the two pie charts below indicate.

■ = **Population living under democratic government***

1990   2008

* Any definition of democracy may carry an element of political bias, and that is certainly the case here, as the judgment is made by the US organization Freedom House.

also a former political prisoner of the US-sponsored Pinochet dictatorship. Elsewhere trade unionists, lower-rank soldiers and a playboy Catholic priest have broken the monopoly of a political class made up of professional politicians, lawyers, entrepreneurs and big landowners. Despite enduring difficulties, the continent is in some ways an exciting departure from the 'strong market/weak democracy' model described in this book. But steps towards equality and economic justice have largely not been accompanied by changes in the political sphere that would spread significant decision-making beyond the centralized nation state.

Even in Africa, home of an often bloated and highly militarized post-colonial state, there are some hopeful signs – the defeat of apartheid in South Africa and the first relatively honest elections for many years in the continent's most populous country, Nigeria. It is a promising start, but otherwise genuinely representative government only clings on in a few countries of the continent's west (Ghana, Senegal) and south (Botswana, Mozambique and Malawi). The north, east and Horn regions are still preyed on by political bosses who would rather fight than switch – continuing electoral manipulation in Kenya, military meddling in Madagascar and the ruthless Bashir Government in Sudan are unfortunately not aberrations but business as usual for this part of the world.

In Asia, meanwhile, representative institutions have gained ground from Pakistan to Cambodia, although in many places they remain fragile and under siege from a number of undemocratic sources. In the Arab world, good democratic examples are still notable by their absence, with the credentials of 'guided' democracies like Mubarak's Egypt or Assad's Syria of decidedly questionable merit.

There are many other signs of an emerging international consensus on the value of representative institutions and respect for at least a minimum of human rights. The World Bank and the International Monetary Fund (IMF) are proposing to punish those whose records on things like 'transparency' and 'good governance' are deemed to be inadequate – a far cry from the days when political and economic stability were the flavor of the month and these two erstwhile champions of democracy turned a blind eye to the corpses in the national stadium in Chile or Indonesia's rivers of blood following the military coup of 1967. This marks a major change. The end of Cold War competition should have taken a lot of the ideological heat and hypocritical posturing out of political debate. There should be a welcome clearing of the air and a return to more honest criteria over 'what is' and 'what isn't' democracy.

Democracy after the Cold War

Since the end of the Cold War it is no longer enough to have to justify a set of political arrangements (whether democratic or not) by reference to an undemocratic and sinister 'other' by simply saying 'things could be a lot worse'. Now democracy or its absence must stand naked on its own and be judged for what it is rather than what it isn't. And it is not just the intelligentsia of politics (political scientists, journalists, pundits and so on) who are now doing the judging but also ordinary citizens. The results of their judgments are quite sobering. For if democracy appears on the one hand never stronger, it is also being subjected to a ground-swell of dissatisfaction from below.

The indicators of this dissatisfaction are everywhere. The decline in voter participation has spread beyond North America (in the US less than 50 per cent of the electorate bothers to vote and the last Canadian elections witnessed the lowest turnout in the country's history). Most non-compulsory European voter participation has dropped significantly over the past 25 years. A study of 15 western European countries found that membership of political parties had declined almost a third – from 8.2 per cent of the electorate in the early 1980s to 5.2 per cent by the mid-1990s.[4]

A survey asking the provocative question 'do politicians care?' showed a steady decline from the mid-1970s to 2004 amongst Swedes and French people and an overall decline punctuated by erratic spikes of enthusiasm amongst US voters. A multi-country survey showed a growing belief that democracy was the best form of government but less support for the idea that it is a good form of government. In the US there was less support for both notions.[5]

You can almost taste the disappointment with democracy in eastern Europe and the countries that made up the former USSR. The same old figures who ran things under the old communist system are now often back, dressed in democratic clothes. The electorate swings erratically between Left and Right looking for the elusive promise of democracy. The old cynicism from below that marked communist rule is now reborn as a reaction to the new political élite that is consolidating power.

Everywhere it is the economically marginal, those with fewer resources (and arguably more to gain from responsive government) who are absenting themselves from the political process. In the UK, for example, only 2.6 per cent of those who own property are not on the electoral register while 38.2 per cent of those living in furnished rental accommodation have never bothered to register.[6] Democratic politics is becoming more a means for the relatively privileged to defend what they have, rather than a vehicle for change based on a more equal vision of society.

Frustrated voters
Even where people still bother to cast their ballots they find the political arrangements in place limit their influence and frustrate their intentions. Systems based on the

Westminster 'first-past-the-post' (FPTP) model (peculiar to the English-speaking world) are particularly bad at reflecting the broad range of political opinions and options. Voters are often caught in the 'lesser-of-two-evils' syndrome. FPTP tends to favor a couple of large, well-funded parties with fairly similar ideologies (in practice if not in rhetoric), which reinforces the general public perception that politicians are 'all the same'. These parties are often referred to as 'brokerage parties' because of their 'all things to all people' approach during election campaigns and their lack of commitment to any clear ideology beyond the pragmatism of power. They bring whatever interests are available into some kind of working arrangement so that ideology takes second place to getting a piece of the action.

Extreme views, populist impulses, new thinking and idiosyncratic figures are all casualties of a bland sameness that pervades this kind of political culture. Brokerage parties (with constantly reworked 'market' solutions) provide a muscular orthodoxy that reinforces this by actively marginalizing outlying ideas. Oddly, this sameness does not lead to civility in political life for, where real policy differences are absent, politics tend to revolve around personality and endless expensive attempts at proving what a lowlife scoundrel the other guy is. Often there is plenty of scandal to uncover, as the absence of ideals means most politicians are attracted to politics for gain and glory.

While there is also a tendency towards this in voting systems based on proportionality (Proportional Representation or PR is the main system of electoral representation in Europe, Latin America and the former Soviet Union) it is far more pronounced under FPTP. Voter turnout is lower and voter dissatisfaction higher under FPTP. Little wonder when a political party can win a 'landslide' mandate with the votes of only 40-odd per cent of those who even bother voting, depending on how the vote splits.

Another way voters find their preferences frustrated is in boundary arrangements that privilege some voters over others. Sometimes this is the result of gerrymandering – the manipulation of political boundaries by the ruling party to gain the best possible results. More typically this situation favors rural voters over their urban counterparts. In Canada, for example, there are some 101 seats (mostly urban) with between 100,000 and 120,000 citizens while 35 others (mostly rural) are decided by between 20,000 and 75,000 voters.[7]

A rural tilt to voting can exercise a conservative influence on political life – clearly seen in countries like France or Germany, or in the US, where senators from sparsely populated western states ensure the defeat of many otherwise popular environmental protection measures.

The conscious exclusion of certain categories of potential voters militates against a really inclusive democracy. While a franchise based on property-holding has fallen out of favor, there are still many categories of exclusion. Migrant workers are excluded almost everywhere and this is particularly unfair, as in parts of Europe they form a significant percentage of the working class and have lived in their 'host' societies for decades. People with criminal records are excluded from voting in some places, including many parts of the US. Since the US imprisons a large percentage of its black male population, this in effect becomes a category of racial exclusion. In those places with elaborate voter registration systems, it is often difficult for the poor and semi-literate to vote. The political rights of women in many states from Sudan to Afghanistan are severely curtailed.

In many cases it is not the lack of the opportunity to vote that is the problem. In the US alone there are estimated to be an astounding 500,000 public officials who need to get elected. Other democracies with hidebound civil service bureaucracies might consider making more positions, particularly local ones, subject to election. But the main predicament facing most democracies is people who exclude themselves from electing candidates. This reflects widely held feelings of apathy and powerlessness. The politicians who are supposed to represent people are often considered distant and unresponsive. They are a class apart from the normal voter. If there is either no contest (one candidate is deemed to be unbeatable) or no significant issue (all candidates support variants of the same policy) this voter apathy is bound to skyrocket.

A study done by US-based Center for Voting and Democracy analyzed a series of Congressional elections and found that voter participation varied between 30 per cent (no contest) and 43 per cent (close call) depending on the competitiveness of the race.[8] So voter participation would be enhanced in contentious elections where there are significant philosophical differences between candidates. Is it surprising then that in most of the industrialized world, where politicians cling to a narrow range of views on the fundamentals of how to run a market economy (privatization, cuts in spending and in taxes, deregulation, incentives to wealthy investors) that so many voters just can't be bothered? Overall voter participation around the world has dropped from a post-World War Two high of 78 per cent (1946) to the 2006 level of 66.5 per cent.[9]

A professional political class

But democracy's malaise goes deeper than the decline in voting and the manipulation of electoral arrangements by a self-serving élite. It stems from the very depths of what we imagine democracy to be. Many still have the lingering sense that democracy means 'rule by the people' – in other words, people participate in the decisions that affect them most closely. If this is the central criterion of a democracy, we are a long way from it now. This sense of a failed promise actually to achieve a democratic life is perhaps the underlying reason for the groundswell of discontent.

Our current systems of democracy – highly centralized governments in which we are 'represented' by a class of professional politicians – seem to have betrayed the promise of self-rule. And while the lack of real choice in competitive candidates and ideas amongst these professional politicians is a part of the malaise, it is hardly the whole picture. The system of centralized state power seems increasingly remote from most people's lives and it becomes difficult to believe that politicians (no matter what their views) concerned with the macro-management of society and economy have any real interest in what is important to us.

This view is reinforced every time a politician tells voters one thing to get elected (they will remove a particular tax, not sign a trade agreement, bring in a new social program) and when they are in power does the exact opposite. While this is often put down to the typical hypocrisy of politicians, it is more than that. It is a go-with-the-flow, do-what-powerful-business-interests-want and don't-rock-the-boat kind of ethos that glues political life together.

A consequence of this is an extraordinary popular hostility to not only the political class but government per se and all its works. Conservative politicians have proved the most adept at harnessing this hostility (often glorifying the 'honest' market at the expense of the 'corrupt' state) and using anti-government rhetoric to achieve, paradoxically, the very positions of power they are attacking. They are even prone to attack 'big government' at the same time as they are cynically using the powers of the state to reward their friends and vanquish their enemies. Juxtaposing the 'choice' offered by the market (with the important caveat that you have the money to exercise this choice) with the lack of any real political choice contributes to the democratic malaise. It is a deceptive sleight of hand that portrays the market as a mechanism of or for democracy. But in a situation of democratic disappointment and alienation from an unaccountable political class the wizardry often goes unnoticed.

The centralization of political power is at work on almost all levels – whatever the champions of the market would have us believe. The big political parties are increasingly remote from the voters. Members at party conventions or conferences see their policy resolutions routinely ignored by those they help elect. The rank-and-file backbench representative who sits in a parliament or national assembly has little control over the cabinet or, if in opposition, the shadow cabinet. The cabinet has less control over the increasingly large office of the chief executive, be they Prime Minister, President or Premier. 'Don't tie our hands' is the cry used all down the line to drown out the sound of breaking promises and abandoned commitments.

We are left with a series of puzzling questions as to why government isn't better at representing the public interest and who is really setting the agenda.

Who gets to the top?

The political class forms a more or less permanent, if sometimes rotating, government élite. The same faces pop up over and over again. The frequency with which we hear about the phenomenon of the 'political come-back' is a good indicator of how difficult it is to get rid of them. Israeli politicians such as Shimon Peres and Benjamin Netanyahu have monopolized political life for decades. Sometimes a figure (like Peres) will serve many political masters and blow with the ideological breezes, shifting gracefully from Left to Right (and sometimes even back again). Perhaps in no other human endeavor is the octogenarian male so prominent. Men in their late seventies and early eighties play a disproportionate role in the governing of many nations. About a quarter of the US Senate is over 70 years of age – all but two of them men.

The kind of people who have already accumulated a high level of economic and social power are usually over-represented in the political class. Lawyers and those from the corporate boardroom tend to predominate. Other professionals are not far behind. Political power is really the preserve of what used to be called the 'better sort of people'.

Groups that are on the 'outs' – blacks and latinos in the US (Obama notwithstanding), Dalits ('untouchables') in India, many types of immigrants, indigenous peoples everywhere – tend to be greatly under-represented. Women have traditionally been excluded and although there is some change here (particularly in northern Europe and, to a lesser degree, South Asia and South Africa) they are also grossly under-represented. Women still make up less than 15 per cent of the members of representative assemblies around the world and the figure drops to well below 10 per cent when it comes to government posts and cabinet-level positions.[10]

Celebrity can itself provide a ticket to power, as with show-business figures such as Ronald Reagan and, more recently, Arnold Schwarzenegger in the US and Joseph Estrada in the Philippines. The 2009 election in the remote Indian state of Bihar pitted a talk-show host against a Bollywood actor. Celebrity-hungry Bulgarians, meanwhile, were desperate enough to elect their former king as Prime Minister. As with most celebrities, these are magical figures who exist in a realm different from our own. The most important ones are surrounded by a security apparatus to ensure they remain untouchable. Security for the powerful has become both an obsession and a multi-billion-dollar business. We are supposed to feel grateful when one of them does a 'streeter', mixing with the crowds and displaying that carefully crafted 'common touch' that

it is so important for professional politicians to cultivate. The recurrence of the same family names speaks
to the continuity in the political class – Kennedy,
Bush, Bhutto, Clinton, Churchill and Gandhi.

Politicians from this governing culture tend to
form a seamless web with those who hold power in
the economy and society more generally. They are
on the same boards, live in the same toney neighborhoods, are members of the same clubs, have their
kids in the same private schools. It is by and large a

Recent progress in women's right to vote

1970: Yemen adopts full suffrage and Andorra permits women to vote.
1971: Switzerland adopts female suffrage, and the US lowers the
      voting age for both men and women to 18.
1972: Bangladesh grants female suffrage.
1973: Women in Bahrain win the vote.
1973: Women are permitted to stand for election in Andorra and San
      Marino.
1974: Jordan and the Solomon Islands extend suffrage to women.
1975: Angola, Cape Verde and Mozambique give women the vote.
1976: Portugal adopts female suffrage with a few restrictions.
1978: The Republic of Moldova adopts full suffrage with a few
      restrictions.
1978: Women in Zimbabwe are now able to stand for election.
1979: Women in the Marshall Islands and Micronesia gain full
      suffrage right.
1980: Iran gives women the vote.
1984: Full suffrage is granted to the women of Liechtenstein, while
      in South Africa voting rights are extended to 'Coloureds' and
      'Indians', including women.
1986: Central African Republic adopts female suffrage.
1990: Samoan women win the vote.
1994: Black women gain full suffrage in South Africa, while women
      in Kazakhstan also win the vote.
2005: Women in Kuwait win the vote.

The only countries where women still have no right to vote are Saudi
Arabia, Brunei (where nobody votes) and the United Arab Emirates
(though this may change in 2010). In Lebanon proof of elementary
education is required for women but not men. In Vatican City only
the Cardinals (all male) get to vote in the election of the Pope. ■

comfortable world, although the pressures of hanging on can be very real. There is a shared ethos of doing things 'properly' – which usually means doing things in ways that do not threaten and if possible enhance the interests of that world.

The former US Vice-President Dick Cheney is a classic example. Cheney is a long-time member of the conservative wing of the US political class who served as Secretary of Defense under Bush senior in the early 1990s. He then moved into private business – a big Dallas-based oil services company called Halliburton. When he first started at Halliburton they were doing less than $300 million of work for the US Defense Department. When he left it was up over $650 million. Paul O'Neill, Treasury Secretary in the Bush Cabinet, and the former chair of Alcoa (the world's largest aluminum company) apparently felt no need to divest himself of his $90-million-plus stock options in that company. As we have already seen, this continuity of well-heeled insiders has continued under Obama. In Russia, the business-cum-criminal class of wealthy oligarchs formed a kind of court around Boris Yeltsin and now Vladimir Putin and his successor Dmitry Medvedev. In Italy, Silvio Berlusconi, one of the country's richest men, who has a stranglehold on much of the Italian media, has used his wealth and influence to make himself one of the leading figures in Italian politics. A kind of 'revolving door' often operates between the political and economic élites, rewarding the former for their services once they leave office. In the Global South, the difference between the circumstances of the political class and that of the ordinary citizenry is even more marked. Their money is often in places where wealth seeks asylum (Switzerland or the Cayman Islands), their children in universities in Australia and the US, their healthcare in Singapore, Europe or North America and their property in Paris or California.

Democratic malaise

Crooked politicians

A revealing way in which politicians have become 'a class apart' is in their belief almost across the political spectrum that they stand *legibus solutus* or 'above the law'. Whether it is illegal wiretapping (François Mitterrand in France) or municipal rake-offs (Jacques Chirac, also in France), personal enrichment (Russia's Boris Yeltsin and Mexico's Carlos Salinas) or evasion of democratic accountability (George W Bush and the illegal surveillance of millions of US citizens), the political class consistently breaks the law for reasons of financial gain or to maintain and protect its own power. Nicaraguan President Daniel Ortega never had to stand trial for the alleged sexual abuse of his step-daughter because of parliamentary immunity.

Politicians are often not caught and seldom prosecuted. Two notable exceptions are President Joseph Estrada of the Philippines, who was caught pilfering the public coffers, and President Carlos Menem of Argentina, who was indicted for illegal arms sales. But often a public apology seems to suffice. In many places, as in Japan, such apologies have become a kind of national rite. The 'sacred trust' of elected office is now almost constantly beset by scandal from Peru to Poland, Canada to Cambodia. The arrogance of power resides in the unstated but persistent conviction that the 'divine right of kings' has been modified into a kind of 'divine right of elected leaders' to flout the law.

Another source of popular alienation from the way democracy is currently practiced has to do with money. There is a pervading sense that money makes democracy dirty. It is estimated that a US presidential election will cost approximately one billion US dollars. Major contributors are seen to be in a good position to exert influence on those whom they help elect. The 2008/09 bailout of the financial industry on both sides of the Atlantic and beyond is some indication of the way the political class is trapped in the logic of 'I'll scratch your back if you scratch mine'.

As party membership declines, politicians must depend more and more on corporate largesse to fund expensive media-based advertising campaigns during elections. The UK Labour Party is a classic case. As the donations of individual donors recede in importance, major corporate donors are filling the gap. This has included everybody from the US fast-food chain McDonald's to Lords Hamlyn and Sainsbury (of supermarket chain fame) who each coughed up £2 million ($3.3 million). In April 2000, the Party held a dinner costing £500 ($835) a plate, where major companies with important stakes in government decisions gobbled up most of the gourmet goodies at the Grosvenor Hotel. No danger here from the 'class enemy' of business.

Money still talks

Various remedies have been proposed and implemented to level the political playing field so that money does not have such a large say. Most of this has been in the form of spending limits and other campaign finance legislation. Such limits have, by and large, been weaker in North America and stronger in their restrictions in Europe and elsewhere. Since this kind of legislation came into effect virtually every major democracy (and a few smaller ones as well) has been rocked by revelations of lawbreaking to avoid campaign finance rules by a major political figure. The best-known case is that of Helmut Kohl, the longtime conservative Chancellor of Germany, who laundered a fortune in illegal campaign contributions and sank the political fortunes of his Christian Democratic Party. But it does not stop there: campaign finance scandals rocked the Clinton Administration in Washington and are almost a monthly occurrence in Japan. Britain's New Labour Government came under attack for its economic dependence on a few key billionaires. Politicians everywhere are caught in the dilemma of how to raise the big bucks needed for political success without appearing to be in the back pocket of wealthy contributors. Campaign finance controls spring from an understandable desire for honesty and fairness. The consistent breaking or evasion of these rules is yet another source of the growing alienation from the dominant political class.

Already Japan's new Prime Minister Yukio Hatoyama, (alias Twinkletoes) has been hit by scandal when it was discovered that some $220,000 came to his campaign from 90 fictitious donors, including dead people. His predecessor Ichiro Ozawa, of the long-dominant Liberal Democratic Party, was forced to resign because of just this kind of issue. Hatoyama's Democratic Party, elected at the end of August 2009, promised (you guessed it) 'change' and 'honesty' but *plus ça change*. It is little wonder that the global political class was so generous in its bail-outs of banks and other wealth-holders. They owed!

What all this campaign money sloshing around does is buy a lot of 'image'. The elaborate machinery of electoral success (pollsters, focus groups, telemarketers, saturation advertising, brain trusts of consultants, hoopla political conventions) have been exported from the US along with Disney movies and Microsoft computer games. The same voters who are alienated by big money politics may be seduced by the image that it buys. Policy and issues of substance shrink in political importance, overshadowed by competing image machines playing on the personal virtues of leaders – strength, integrity and so on. A classic proof is a directive leaked by a British Labour Party MP which came from the Party leadership in the run-up to a national election. The 'good members' were told to spend a maximum of 30 seconds talking to their constituents and that they should not engage in prolonged discussion with anyone about Party policy. So much for representation and sober reflection. Turbo-capitalism is throwing up a politics whose democracy is a matter of show business that has abandoned any real interest in popular sovereignty.

Uploading power
Centralization of power into the hands of a narrow political élite doesn't just take place within political parties or national governments. It is happening at all levels of governance. Centralization is sucking the vitality from regional, municipal and local government where their powers (particularly over the raising of money through taxation) are being usurped by national politicians. Thus the levels of government closest to people are left with the least power to shape policy and defend the quality of life. They often have no constitutional existence of their own, instead owing their legal arrangements to the whim of governments 'above' them. Such 'superior' governments think nothing of intervening to change electoral arrangements, eliminate mayors, redraw municipal boundaries and even eliminate whole levels of government. Power is often reduced while responsibilities are increased. The term 'downloading' has been coined to describe the phenomenon of the national state shedding responsibilities – but rarely the resources needed to meet them – to local levels of government. Local government is a key provider of many popular government services (recreation, public space, welfare, local environment, local policing, much of public health, housing and homelessness, education in some places) while national states retain the bulk of the resources to fund national programs and the trappings of state (the security apparatus, the foreign service, and the elaborate protocol machine). It is not hard to figure out in this dynamic of centralization where programs are most vulnerable to cost-cutting measures.

Democratic malaise

As if this were not enough, even nation-states are now subjected to pressures from institutions buttressed almost entirely from public democratic pressure; institutions such as the International Monetary Fund (IMF) and the World Trade Organization (WTO). These are the semi-official bodies that enforce the shifting rules of the globalizing economy. The concentration of power in their hands and that of private actors in the global economy (transnational corporations, capital markets, stockholders, currency speculators, bond-rating agencies) has led to an explosion of social-science literature pondering the future of the nation-state. This literature tries (from widely differing points of view) to come to terms with a world in which the once sacrosanct sovereignty of (at least powerful) nation-states is now being hemmed in by economic forces that severely limit economic policy choices.

Nor are restrictions limited to purely economic matters. Such things as government-supported health policies, workplace health and safety, public support for the arts and environmental safeguards all potentially come under a regime of international trade regulations adjudicated and enforced outside the parameters of national legislation. In practical terms this could result in public policy that was supported by the vast majority of citizens (outlawing a polluting additive in gasoline, say, or support for domestic film production) being overruled because it did not fit with a series of international trade and investment rules.

The implications for even the limited amount of democratic choice we still have are obvious enough. The rules are by and large ones that favor market solutions and the interests of transnational corporations (rather than, say, public investment or a government-supported co-operative sector). In other words they empower individual and corporate efforts to maximize private incomes and profits and rule out our collective discussion and decision about the kind of cities, towns and societies we live in.

The opinions in the flood of writing on 'the crisis of the nation-state' stretch from those who celebrate the much-needed discipline the wholesome market imposes on 'unrealistic' democratic aspirations to those appalled by the threat to popular sovereignty. Different theorists give different weightings to this 'drag effect' of globalization on the public-policy decisions of supposedly sovereign governments; none however dispute its existence or its continued growth.

In conclusion, it is fair to say that representative institutions are becoming (with important exceptions) the norm in various parts of the world. But at the same time there is a growing citizen alienation with the 'actually-existing democracies'. This is in part due to the tendencies towards political élitism and manipulation built into the conventional practice of politics, but also to the centralization that sucks power from the local into ever less accountable realms of the political stratosphere. The alienation has a positive side, however: it means there is a lingering sense that democracy could and should be more. The rest of this book will endeavor to explain how we arrived at this tepid commitment to democracy and evaluate the potentials for a more robust version.

1 'None Dare Call it Stolen', Mark Crispin Miller, *Harpers*, August 2005. 2 'Obama at Manassas', Mike Davis, *New Left Review*, March/April 2009. 3 'Why Democrats Can't Govern', Jonathan Chait, *New Republic*, 15 April 2009. 4 *1999 Democracy Forum Report*, Institute for Democracy and Electoral Assistance, Stockholm. 5 Colin Hay, *Why we hate politics*, Polity Press 2007. 6 Democratic Audit, Charter 88, London 1997. 7 Democracy Watch, Ottawa. 8 'This Time Let the Voters Decide', Rob Richie and Steven Hill, in *Making Every Vote Count*, ed Henry Milner, Broadview Press, Peterborough 1999. 9 www.idea.com 10 Inter-Parliamentary Union and the UN Division for the Advancement of Women.

3 Weak and strong democracy

'In democracy you can be respected though poor, but don't count on it.'
Charles Merrill Smith, writer.

Two strains can be identified in the history of democratic thought and experience. One is a weak democracy where popular sovereignty is hemmed in by the individual right to property that holds sway over the collective rights of the community. This theory is based on a notion of possessive individualism and is a strong market/weak democracy model. The second strain is the notion of strong democracy rooted in the radical republican tradition, which emphasizes the self-rule of the political community and the equality of power in democratic decision-making.

EVEN AT DEMOCRACY's birth, its critics were present and vocal. Plato and many others greeted its appearance in ancient Athens with grave warnings about entrusting the well-being of the city to an unpredictable mob. He was not alone in opposing the direct involvement of the whole body of citizens in its own self-government. He and many others preferred a politics firmly in the grip of 'the better sort', experts in the specific knowledge of politics (comparable to today's political class). Athenian democracy (a direct democracy of rich and poor alike but excluding women and slaves) had its champions as well. Protagoras, a friend and adviser to the influential Pericles, held that any adult citizen was capable of acquiring the art of politics (the ability to make reasoned judgments on the city's affairs) and should therefore be part of the body deciding these issues. Even Aristotle, another critic of full democracy, thought that a person became fully human only by taking part in politics. The Greek notion of the 'idiot' meant someone ignorant of public affairs. Thousands of Athenian citizens would gather to debate and decide on the issues of the day.

As democratic activist/theorist C Douglas Lummis points out, 'while the Athenians did not invent slavery and patriarchy (or empire for that matter), neither did they abolish them; what they did do was to discover public freedom'.[1] Looking back from the 19th century, the political philosopher John Stuart Mill held that the Athenian achievement of a substantial degree of citizen self-government 'raised the intellectual standards of an average Athenian citizen far beyond anything of which there is yet an example in any other mass of men, ancient or modern'.[2]

After the collapse of the Athenian and later the Roman republics, the intellectual debate as to the merits of democracy faded. But this did not curtail people's efforts to control their own circumstances and fate. The democratic impulse has been widespread across time and place – taking a multitude of forms in different early societies, religious movements, artisan guilds, monastic communities and in a rich variety of peasant revolts. Heretical sects, such as the Albigensians or Cathars in the south of France and the dissenting movements of eastern Europe, resisted the power of both the central Church and the State. The democratic impulse both predates and coexists with more elaborated theories of democracy and acts as a constant pressure to push the limits of 'actually existing democracies' in both theory and practice.

This democratic impulse cannot be claimed by the West in the way it claims the formal liberal-democratic tradition as being rooted in the philosophy of the Enlightenment and the practice of the American and French Revolutions. It is more widely cast in the struggles of peasant villages against landlords and warlords, indigenous peoples against enemies of an egalitarian way of life, independent peoples against expanding empires, religious dissenters against power-wielding clerics and even the rebellions of youth against domination by elders. Anthropologists disagree as to when, where and why a power separate from society crystallized in the form of a hierarchy. But perhaps a buried memory of a time before state and kingship is the original source of the democratic impulse.

Possessive individualism

Thinking about democracy as a system of government that is a contract between ruler and ruled starts to emerge only in the 16th and 17th centuries. But these theorists of a government based on the consent (of at least some) of the governed – the Hobbes, Mills, Lockes, even the more radical Rousseaus and Jeffersons – were also deeply ambivalent about the foundational meaning of democracy as 'rule by the people'. In the original Greek, democracy is the kratos of the demos – the power of the people. But by the 17th century this had to be reconciled with a large number of anti-democratic structures: monarchies, aristocracies, slavery, patriarchy and the emergence of a class of wealthy property owners. The dreamers of the new democratic freedom were almost all haunted by nightmares of 'mob rule' and the overthrow of property. As Ireton, the Roundhead leader Cromwell's right-hand man, cautioned the uppity Levellers, who had been inspired by the ideals of the English Revolution to want a more profound democracy, 'liberty cannot be provided for in a general sense if property is (to be) preserved'.

So the original thinkers and theorists of a liberal democracy drew back from the precipice and judged that only men with a certain amount of property could be trusted with the exercise of consent (the vote). This limited notion of a liberal democracy, particularly associated with John Locke and James Mills, has been dubbed by the political philosopher CB Macpherson as a 'theory of possessive individualism'. Those without property were seen by definition as irresponsible (lacking a stake in society) and thus had to be excluded from citizenship. Even for those who had the vote, elections were to be for 'representatives' who would govern in their stead. Such 'representation' was assumed quite indirect, with the Member of Parliament retaining as much independence as was necessary for political stability and good order. This was a negative kind of consent – a freedom from arbitrary rule rather than a freedom to rule ourselves.

In his work, Macpherson traces this notion of freedom as it evolved out of older forms of obligation and hierarchy. He outlines 'possessive individualism' as follows:

1 The human essence is to use our capacities in search of our satisfactions.

2 Society is no longer a set of relations of feudal domination but a lot of free, equal individuals related to each other through their possessions.

3 Political life is about the protection of these possessions – all capacities, including life and liberty, are considered 'possessions' rather than social rights and obligations. The rights to the use of property are thus fundamental.[3]

This notion of liberal democracy has less to do with methods of collective decision-making than with the protection of the individual from arbitrary interference. Those with more property obviously had more to lose and needed more protection from arbitrary interference. On the question of the arbitrary interference by those with more property against those with less, possessive individualism was silent. Thus liberalism was not inherently democratic – in fact it was hostile to the notion of full democracy.

Origins of weak democracy
This is the basis for the 'weak' notion of democracy that is still with us – that a minimalist state should interfere as little as possible with the economic and political rights of individuals. The then-emerging

market is seen as a more-or-less natural way of ordering human affairs. But it must as much as possible be left to its own devices. It is not hard to see in this early 'possessive individualism' the kernel of contemporary arguments now fashionable with the New Right. Get government off our backs! Don't shackle wealth! Roll back government through a process of privatization, tax cuts, deregulation and so forth. Allow for the 'natural' operation of the market. Individual rights outweigh the collective democratic decisions of society. The former British Prime Minister Margaret Thatcher even went so far as to deny the very existence of society.

The emphasis of early liberalism (the democratic part came later) was on 'choice'. As Macpherson summarizes it: 'Instead of a society based on custom, and on status, and on authoritarian allocation of work and rewards, you have a society based on individual mobility, on contract and on impersonal market allocation of work and rewards in response to individual choices. Everyone was swept into the free market.'

In this market society the ideology of choice was extended to the political system and a limited number of voters: 'The electorate need not be a democratic one, and as a general rule was not; all that was needed was an electorate consisting of men of substance, so that the government would be responsive to their choices.'[4]

Another cultural strain of conservatism, associated with the British conservative Edmund Burke and the French Alexis de Tocqueville, projected a fear of the poor mob that threatened to topple the 'better sort' of people. The right to vote denied to the mass of people then became a major focus of democratic struggles. Working-class and feminist campaigners made the logical case that women and people without property were citizens too. These were long hard struggles, involving many dashed hopes and not a few dashed bodies. Many democratic activists devoted their lives to this fight.

It was not until the late 19th and early 20th century (several hundred years after the painful birth of liberal society in the English Revolution) that the battle to extend the democratic franchise to all adults was gradually achieved. But such struggles continued right up through the early 1960s' civil rights movement to enfranchise black people in the southern US and indeed to this day as different groups (immigrants, poor people, former prisoners, various minority groups) continue to be excluded from voting. But despite the extension of the right to vote, the system of weak democracy still privileged those with enough wealth to shape and influence 'democratic outcomes'.

A strong democracy

From the earliest days of democratic thinking and development there emerges a struggle between a *weak* notion of democracy and a *stronger* version. It has continued to the present day. Early proponents of strong popular democracy were firebrands such as Thomas Paine, and radical theorists such as Jean-Jacques Rousseau. The French republican movement and advocates of early working-class politics such as the English Chartists and radical artisan movements across Europe continued to push the limits of market/ property democracy. When the suffragist movement and various civil rights movements picked up the torch, they were advocating not merely the vote in national elections but also the extension of democratic equality into the family and the economy.

The notion of a strong democracy was propelled forward by the popular democratic impulse and the constant threat of democratic outbreaks from below. It found its intellectual reflection in a diversity of radical democratic ideas. The propertied and conservative establishment in turn pushed back and tried to reduce democratic space. Those with power

Strong democracy: the urban crucible

'Who do you call when your toilet backs up?' This old political adage is a way of pointing out which level of government is most important to most people. Who do you depend on for physical security? Public health? Housing standards? Recreational facilities? Cultural amenities? Survival income when there is no other? It is usually the city or town council or whatever local authority exists. Granted many still do not have a toilet to back up (to say nothing of income). But the point remains valid that, whether it is a village in rural India, a shantytown on the edge of São Paulo or an industrial suburb of Marseille, it is the local which is often crucial. As another old political sage put it, 'all democracy is local'.

This sounds good in principle but it seems to be losing out in practice. Almost everywhere, centralizing nation-states are sucking power away from the local. A market-oriented agenda of cutbacks, privatization and 'economic rationalization' of local government is taking its toll. Municipal government is being reduced to a powerless 'service delivery' unit. A democratic deficit is being built up at the local level – with higher levels of government limiting the means to provide services while increasing the number of services to be provided.

In Toronto, Canada's largest city, the Conservative provincial government has redrawn municipal boundaries, creating a city that no longer recognizes itself. Local self-governing municipalities were merged into a remote supercity. The number of local representatives elected has been dramatically cut. Torontonians resisted this move, voting some 70 per cent in a referendum to reject it. The provincial government simply ignored the results and reshaped the city according to its cost-cutting whims. Without any legal, constitutional status, local democracy was at the mercy of central authority. And Toronto is not alone. The centralization of power away from the local and towards the regional is most visible amongst the world's burgeoning super-cities. Over the past quarter century these kinds of 'rationalization' of local government have hit everywhere from London to New York. Budgets have been slashed, powers reduced, mayoralties removed and then brought back. The ability to raise revenue locally has been severely restricted. With the municipal government at the sharp end of a number of vital issues, from homelessness and poverty to public transport and environmental deterioration, the loss has been not only to local democracy but to the quality of urban life.

But the centralizers have not had it all their own way. In Toronto, the organization Citizens for Local Democracy has been waging a lively fight to revitalize grassroots power. It now forms a network with a number of other organizations such as the Bread Not Circuses

Coalition (resisting the city's Olympic bid), the Toronto Environmental Alliance and other activist groups working around homelessness, transit, tenants' rights, and a plethora of other issues that shape the quality of urban life. Together they put forward an alternative vision of what the city might be like if it controlled its own fate.

You can find similar struggles going on in nearly every major urban area. Cities across the globe have become points of resistance to the centralizing ambitions of the national political class. Back in the 1980s, places like Bologna in Italy and Kyoto in Japan were models of cities whose approach to a balanced development involved a significant degree of popular empowerment rather than simply turning things over to the real-estate lobby. More recently cities such as London (where the independent mayoral candidate Ken Livingstone won power in 2000), Mexico City (where the center-left opposition PRD party holds power) and now Paris (Delanoë) and Berlin (Wowereit), have taken up the fight to assert their own agendas and priorities in the face of a national state concerned more with cost-cutting and privatization than with providing the public goods necessary for a decent quality of urban life. Cities, particularly big cities, are potential building blocks of a strong democracy.

Cities and towns are often exciting sites of democratic experimentation. In the center of Copenhagen the alternative community of Christiania's use of self-government through direct popular participation is one example – a troublesome one for the Danish national state now trying to impose 'normalization' on this youth culture enclave. The Japanese seaport of Maki, meanwhile, has used local referenda to frustrate the plans of the powerful National Nuclear Agency. If this has happened in highly centralized Japan, one can imagine the potential in societies like Thailand or Catalonia in Spain where local resistance to central power is the main currency of politics.

So, with the majority of the world's population moving into cities, it is heartening to see a growing municipal countertrend of resistance and experimentation in the face of a power-hungry national political class. This is particularly true as the nation-state mortgages local democratic rights (especially over economic issues) to the heavy hand of trade liberalization agreements administered by the World Trade Organization. Of course, democratic forms will vary from smallish towns in the industrial Global North to the poor communities that surround Lagos in Nigeria or Lima in Peru. But all local forms have greater potential to be animated by the original democratic ideal that it is up to people themselves to decide. After all, it was in the urban crucible of ancient Athens, the Italian city-states, philosopher Jean-Jacques Rousseau's Geneva and the 1871 Paris Commune that many of our received notions of a strong democracy were forged. ■

and privilege engage in a constant struggle to rein in democratic expectations and possibilities, seeing this as essential to maintain their rights in the market and their ability to manage the state. In shifting historical and geographic contexts this struggle continues.

Macpherson believes that the original theory of property-based democracy reflected the real economic conditions of a then-emerging capitalism. The notion of equality based on a 'republic of smallholders' (farmers, artisans, small-business people) had some reality several centuries ago. But the theory has not kept up with the reality. The modern economy, dominated by a couple of thousand transnational corporations and banks, is a virtual economic dictatorship of global proportions. The response of the dominant stream of theory has been to abandon the idea that inequality of property had any political relevance. The right to vote and to protection of the laws was extended to all, whatever their economic power. Thus the theory of liberal democracy was adjusted to defend the legitimacy of the extraordinary inequality of wealth and privilege that we see today.

Ratifying weak democracy

Most conventional political science has adopted the property-blind theory of liberal democracy as the one and only theory of democracy. Theorists devise prescriptions for weak democracy and the empirical attend to the mechanics of how systems in richer countries generally work and how poorer countries can bring their systems into line. They by and large eschew judgments about how democratic this model actually is. So critical political philosophy and theory are displaced by detailed descriptions of how interest group competition works or comparisons of various constitutional arrangements.

Modern political and social science has clearly inherited a distrust of ordinary people and their capacities to participate in their own self-government. Most political scientists stress questions of political management and the comparative effectiveness of various élite systems of government. Participation (except passively during elections) is not to be encouraged. Stability and the equilibrium of the system are held as higher values than participation and popular empowerment. The tilt is clearly towards a weak democracy.

This reflected the major intellectual currents that had gained predominance by the early 20th century. Sociologists like the German Max Weber focused on bureaucracy as the key to understanding the working of modern management systems. Others, like the Swiss Michels and the Italians Mosca and Pareto, formed a school of classic élite theorists and put forward an almost 'iron law of oligarchy'. This postulated (or rather insisted) that democracy was undermined by the inevitable rise of an élite in any complex organization, whether a modern political party or a government. Pessimism about democratic possibilities became the norm. As the political economist Joseph Schumpeter famously concluded: 'Voters must understand that once they have elected an individual, political action is his business and not theirs. This means that they must refrain from instructing him about what he is to do.'[5]

The power of the people was plainly off the agenda. Political thinkers such as Walter Lippmann in the US became much more concerned with the politics of mass persuasion (manipulation) than with the niceties of democratic rule. Perhaps the classic modern statement in favor of weak democracy is captured by the British Conservative Prime Minister Winston Churchill when he proclaimed that 'democracy is the worst form of government except all those other forms that have been tried from time to time'. Faint praise indeed. A recent revealing, if somewhat crude, statement of the weak democracy position concluded The Trouble with Democracy, a lengthy tome by the Canadian conservative William D Gairdner. He believes we need to 'reclaim and revivify democracy with true classic liberalism and once again restore a rule of formal, as distinct from substantive, equality... defend the social and moral hierarchy, and the inequalities this produces, as natural to, and a mark of all free and spontaneous societies...'[6] In other words, because inequality is written into human nature, democracy can in no way be allowed to threaten accumulated wealth and power – even if that wealth and power appears to violate democratic principles.

The Left abandons democracy

The main current of opposition to élitist theories of democracy came from the socialist Left. But the socialists, particularly those of the orthodox Marxist persuasion, have fumbled the democratic ball. They originally focused on overturning the dictatorship in the market and thus replacing Macpherson's 'possessive individualism' with a more broad-based citizenship. In the 19th and early 20th century no-one questioned that the Left stood for a broader, more inclusive democracy – although many questioned whether this was possible or desirable. But the Left, too, abandoned democratic theory. As orthodox Marxism gained ascendancy on the Left it brought with it the assumption that once the market inequalities that undermined democracy were overcome, the self-rule of the workers would automatically emerge. Eventually the state and politics with it would 'wither' away and be replaced by a very technocratic-sounding 'administration of things' to use Marx's compatriot Friedrich Engels' phrase.

There was no need to work out the details of how this self-rule would operate and socialists took little interest in any theory of popular sovereignty that would act as a guarantee for a broader democracy. Indeed any such attempts were denounced as utopian. In hindsight these flaws proved fatal. With the first

Soviet leader Lenin's autocratic adaptation of Marxism into a one-party rule – 'dictatorship of the proletariat' – ideas of workers' self-government receded into the far-distant future.

Under Lenin's successor Stalin and later leaders, the Soviet Union ossified into an autocratic state structure with an unresponsive and increasingly inefficient command economy. This police-state approach to socialism and economic development gave away the Left's best argument. The natural advocates of a strong democracy had abandoned the field. Now the champions of the weak version of market-based democracy could point their fingers in horror at Soviet dictatorship and claim the exclusive democratic franchise. They became the only democratic game in town.

So both sides of the political spectrum are caught trying to reconcile (or denying the need to reconcile) the democratic power of the people with two fundamentally undemocratic structures – the market and the state. In the process, democratic possibilities have atrophied and political thinking about democracy has stagnated. The revival of critical thinking that was sparked by the rise of the 1960s' New Left started to break this down. Some thinkers – such as Herbert Marcuse and European Marxists André Gorz and Henri Lefebvre – sought a human agency to break the deadlock of weak democracy. Others in the Global South, such as Franz Fanon and Amilcar Cabral, sought ways of uprooting the colonial legacy of autocracy. But their emphasis was on liberation and not on how a radical democracy might actually work.

Outbreaks of democracy
The end of the Cold War has created fertile ground for rethinking the fate of democratic ideals. There is now a rekindling of interest in democratic theory and practice that goes beyond the stalemate of state socialism and market-based weak democracy. It has

been the consistent pressure of a democratic impulse from below and the continual 'democratic outbreaks' that it stimulates that have kept democratic practice and ideals on the political agenda.

In a thoughtful essay, the political scientist Ricardo Blaug describes the nature of contemporary democratic outbreaks and how these differ from the various versions of institutionalized democracy. He stresses the episodic nature of these outbreaks and the way they transform passive spectators and consumers of politics into active agents creating informal networks and other forms of democratic action. In moments of political excitement people 'fly to the assemblies', in Rousseau's memorable phrase. Blaug concludes that 'democracy as a way of life has always been highly opportunistic'. It mushrooms into the political space vacated by the loss of order. Crisis, systemic breakdown, incompetent leadership all favor its spread. Examples of democratic outbreaks, some on a massive scale, are common in the history of religious struggles, agricultural uprisings, labor movements and secessionist rebellions. Such challenges have an unexpected and dramatic nature. Blaug explains: 'Trained perhaps by generations of sovereigns and clerics, we now concentrate our attention exclusively on political and cultural élites, and so cannot see the political activity which at last expresses itself in an outbreak of democracy.'[7]

Blaug identifies movements throughout the last century: everything from the spontaneous Danish resistance to the Nazis (yellow stars decorated the coats of tens of thousands of Danes in solidarity with the country's Jews) to the outbreaks of opposition to the Vietnam War, the formation of Solidarity in Poland and the revolt in Paris in 1968. Such revolts are sometimes local, provoked by an environmental outrage (an oil spill, nuclear power accident, or other toxic mishap) or by a particularly abusive act on the part of our political and economic managers. Outbreaks can redefine the political landscape as did the revolutions of 1848 that swept Europe and put absolutist monarchy on notice. Such outbursts are almost inherently critical of weak democracy and push towards a more robust, participatory form of democratic life.

These outbreaks can last hours or years but they provide the constant threat of popular agitation from below – a threat that haunts the political class. They occur, perhaps most profoundly and dangerously, in situations where the denial of democracy is blatant. We can see them at work all over the Global South: the *force populaire* in Haiti risked the Ton Ton Macoutes death squads in the streets of Port-au-Prince... the East Timorese in their decades-long resistance to the Indonesian jackboot... the Chechens in their seemingly hopeless bravery in the face of Moscow's tanks... the Burmese in their intransigent opposition to military rule... Pakistani lawyers in their robes defending the integrity of the legal system... Iranians on the rooftops of Tehran demanding transparent elections and the end of meddling by the theocratic Council of Guardians. In such places autocrats can be overthrown (or else would-be democrats slaughtered) and a situation of democratic possibility can last for weeks or even years before some hardening of possibility into more-or-less 'representative' structures takes place.

These exciting times of political ferment – the Paris Commune in the 1870s, the people's revolutions of eastern Europe in 1989, Portugal after the overthrow of fascism, the Tiananmen Square Movement in Beijing, Barcelona during the Spanish Civil War – were grand outbreaks and are in some sense the real stuff of democracy. They are at once messy, stimulating, full of citizen engagement and hope. Some have grand historic sweep and shift structures and memories inalterably. But they also occur on a less dramatic level around a thousand causes and grievances – citizens who resist the weakening of local government authority by the national state... people who won't tolerate the closing of the neighborhood school or the pushing through of a large highway... people who rally to the defense of a besieged park or to halt the abuse of a local ecosystem due to dumping of toxic wastes or indiscriminate industrial logging.

These democratic outbreaks are the raw material of a transformation of either autocracy or weak democracy into something deeper and more profound. In a situation where a stronger democracy has channels of popular pressure, such initiatives have more chance of success. A weak democracy tilts the odds in favor of the managers of the system and their ability to

Strong democracy: Korea's social movements

'We have no place to go from here.' These words are spoken by Nam Sang-wa, deputy-chairperson of the tenants' committee in Pynchong-dong, part of the bigger Bongchun-dong area of southeast Seoul. A dozen or so tenants are gathered in a living room in one of the houses that has so far escaped the wrecker's ball. Kids run in and out of the room, sitting on their parents' laps until they get restless from too much grown-up talk. And talk there is a-plenty. It swirls around them as they pass the verbal baton from one to the other to explain how the mechanics of property speculation affect poor people.

These are country people who have moved to Seoul in the last few years. On the hillside areas of greater Bongchun-dong poor people are making their last stand in a city rapidly being gobbled up by expensive high-rises. Too many people are chasing too little housing on increasingly expensive land. Absentee house-owners in Pynchong-dong sold out to a development company that, with government approval, has hired a demolition company to destroy their community. Already 75 per cent of the people have been forced out.

But some 134 households are determined to stay. They hold rallies – and drum festivals like the one that happened the previous evening. The demolition company, for its part, turns out the street lights and sets small fires. One of the tenants points to a house 100 meters down the road where some heavy-looking, tattooed guys are hanging out. He says they are members of street gangs the company has hired to harass people as they move up and down the hill.

The Pynchong-dong struggle is no isolated one. The tenants estimate that there are five major redevelopment zones in Seoul and some 500 different struggles to resist forced removal. Such 'quiet heroisms' re-establish order and reassert market forces.

But it is the democratic impulse – people's unquenchable notion that in a democracy they should get to decide – that is always the wild card. It is never obvious when this sense will be violated and the political apple cart will be overturned or at least be made to teeter precariously. The Prime Minister of Japan surely must have been surprised at the public outrage simply because he didn't let the news of a Japanese fishing boat sunk by a US nuclear sub upset his round of golf. Whoever would have thought this would result in the end of his political career? Or how about the Canadian Government's decision to provide

have seen the democratic movement in South Korea through some pretty rough times. Korean social movements are highly organized affairs. They have local chapters and national offices, alliances and coalitions, executives and minutes. Files are neatly stacked, membership payments charted on walls. The residents of Pynchong-dong are connected to the Roomers' Association, which is part of the Association of Urban Poor. This has some 80,000 members and is fighting for the rights of tenants, for decent daycare, and for street vendors who strive to create a life in the cracks of the Korean economy. These vendors add dynamism to Seoul's streets – whether they are selling huge juicy pears or setting up portable bars where one can sit and wash down a variety of seafood snacks. But they have become the latest target of the state's obsession with control from above. Restrictive zoning laws are being used to sweep them away.

Seoul's urban movements fight for the democratic space that will allow citizenship to flourish even in the most unlikely nooks and crannies of urban life. Implicit (and sometimes explicit) in their struggles is the notion of a strong democracy that moves beyond the ballot box. A democracy based on the notion that people have a right to control their own communities and protect their own ways of making a living. These urban struggles are connected to a tradition of militant defense of their rights by both workers and farmers. This has made Korea the site of some of the most combative struggles from below against the ravages of corporate globalization and for a strong democracy. It has also meant a bad reputation in the business press that refers to the last decade (1998-2008) as the 'lost decade' due to this continued combativeness in the face of plans to reassert the strong market/weak democracy model. ∎

millions in financial aid to professional hockey teams so that they could meet the salary demands of the local ice gladiators? There was no reason to think that this corporate giveaway would not be accepted, as many others had been before, and meet with the usual shrugs of resignation. But, after three days of popular outrage, the Government was forced into an embarrassing climbdown.

Several years earlier, the recalcitrant Canadian public had rejected a top-down proposal (put to them in a referendum) to renew the Constitution, even though almost the entire political class was united behind it. Or, more recently, the electorates of France, Holland and Ireland, which rejected the EU's new corporate-friendly constitution despite support from across the political class. No problem – make some minor tinkering changes and pass it without popular ratification except in Ireland where a referendum turned out to be a constitutional necessity. On occasion this kind of popular reaction can sweep across entire continents – as the revulsion to genetically modified foods swept across Europe, to the dismay of Monsanto et al. But questions still hang in the air – are these outbreaks by their very nature episodic? Can we find a way to build on them, to learn from them in order to deepen democracy?

The governability crisis

Some years ago, orthodox political science started to worry about 'the governability of democracy' – the concept comes from the influential Harvard intellectual Samuel Huntington (also an adviser to Richard Nixon on the Vietnam War). Huntington's research (funded by the élite Trilateral Commission) advanced the notion that the system of government was being 'overloaded' with unrealistic popular demands for economic security and political input. In other words, *too much* democracy. Ways needed to be devised to protect the political class, to insulate them from popular pressure. Otherwise how could they make those tough unpopular decisions that were necessary to maintain stability and prosperity?

This was accomplished in a number of key areas. Some decisions, particularly those to do with economic policy, were either left to market forces to negotiate or put in the hands of powerful multilateral agencies like the World Trade Organization or the International Monetary Fund. In both cases they were safely beyond the reach of democratic pressure. A regime of privatization and cutbacks is being deployed to dissuade a 'spoilt' population from the notion that they are entitled to any but the most shoddy of public goods. Anything better will have to be purchased from the lucrative private sector by those who can afford it.

An elaborate national security state has gradually taken shape, to 'police' democracy and protect politicians both personally and politically. So now, when social movements seek to expand democratic space, they can be closely monitored and curtailed if they seek to use the 'illegitimate' means of street politics to advance their cause. A kind of constant low-intensity war, that pays little attention to democratic niceties, is waged against dissidents in many places. Disinformation (sometimes dressed up as public relations) is used to discredit them and invalidate their concerns. The security services deploy a wide range of snooping technologies that contribute to an elaborate national-security state with an inbuilt bias against those advocating change. The 'policing' approach is also extended to parts of the population considered either troublesome or not socially productive. Welfare provision is tied to policing the poor and forcing them into the lowest-paid sectors of the labor market through benefit cuts and workfare schemes. Prison populations are on the rise as the behavior of various ethnic minorities, immigrant groups and youth are criminalized through the use of repressive drug laws. This combination of economic discipline and repressive policing is the current formula for sustaining weak democracy.

Reasserting democracy

But unease with this type of weak democracy is growing – and not just at the grassroots. Major financiers such as George Soros, media czars like Ted Turner and other global luminaries, who meet every year at the famous (now besieged with demonstrators) Swiss resort town of Davos for the World Economic Forum, are starting to express concern that the present weak democracy approach – with its attendant inequalities of wealth and power – is causing a crisis of legitimacy for the system as a whole. Robert Dahl, the dean of democracy studies, now holds that the very pluralism he once championed is being endangered by the power of corporate money swamping the political system.[8]

Dahl thinks that, while market capitalism may initially help in the democratization of some poor countries, it eventually rebounds to undermine that democracy: 'When authoritarian governments in less modernized countries undertake to develop a dynamic market economy, they are likely to sow the seeds of their own ultimate destruction. But once society and politics are transformed by market capitalism and democratic institutions are in place, the outlook fundamentally changes. Now the inequalities in resources that market capitalism churns out produce serious political inequalities amongst citizens.'[9]

Dahl now believes that it is essential to reorganize the economy on democratic principles. Others, such as the British political thinker David Held, are proposing policies to extend democracy beyond the nation-state into the international domain so as to bring democratic pressure to bear on the forces and agencies of globalization previously beyond the reach of popular assemblies and elected officials.[10] From the grassroots, meanwhile, the global justice movement is developing a challenge to the idea of globalization based on reasserting democratic values. Other thinkers and democratic activists have put forward a range of proposals to strengthen democracy in the face of its obvious hijacking by the political class. So the tussle between weak and strong democracy is not about to disappear. It is being recast in contemporary terms, around issues of globalization and economic equality, and more democratic outbursts are just over the horizon.

There are many positive signs that the stagnation in democratic political thought is coming to an end. The concern with 'liberation' that accompanied the 1960s' outbreaks is now shifting to one that explores the ways in which the exercise of popular power can actually shape social decisions. The trick will be to ride this ferment of movements and ideas and use it to effect a long-term transformation that institutionalizes popular power and underpins a strong democracy. The following chapters will explore the potential for this in a number of key areas.

1 C Douglas Lummis, *Radical Democracy*, Cornell University Press, Ithaca 1976. 2 Michael Raptis, *Socialism, Democracy and Self-Management*, Allison and Busby; London 1980. 3 CB Macpherson, *Democratic Theory: Essays in Retrieval*, Clarendon Press, Oxford 1973. 4 CB Macpherson, *The Real World of Democracy*, Canadian Broadcasting Corporation, 1975. 5 Anthony Arblaster, *Democracy*, University of Minnesota Press, Minneapolis 1987. 6 William D Gairdner, *The Trouble with Democracy*, Stoddard, Toronto 2001. 7 Ricardo Blaug, 'Outbreaks of Democracy', *Socialist Register 2000*, Merlin Press, London 2000. 8 RA Dahl, *A Preface to Economic Democracy*, Polity Press, Cambridge 1985. 9 Robert Dahl, *On Democracy*, Yale University Press, New Haven 2000. 10 David Held, *Democracy and the Global Order*, Polity Press, Cambridge 1985.

4 Democratizing the economy

'To discuss democracy without considering the economy in which that democracy is to function is an operation worthy of an ostrich.'
Adam Przeworski, sociologist.

The lack of democracy in economic life undermines democracy everywhere else. Those with economic power – today largely major transnational corporations and banks – have myriad ways to get what they want out of the democratic process. A prerequisite for a more robust democracy is a coherent strategy to level economic and thus political inequalities. This chapter looks at entrenched economic power and evaluates the different strategies for challenging it.

FOR MOST PEOPLE the eight-odd hours (or more in many cases) spent at work have more to do with dictatorship than with democracy. While some workplaces have grown more relaxed, the majority of them still closely monitor your time and what you do with it. When you arrive. When you leave. How you perform your tasks. How long you take for lunch. How many times you go to the bathroom. Whom you talk to on the phone. The demeanor you adopt for your employer. All can be prescribed in some detail, whether you work as a security guard in Berlin or in a fast-food franchise in Seoul, a *maquiladora* clothing factory in Central America or making circuitboards in Penang. This most basic experience of life, earning your livelihood, involves the surrender of both your time and your will to the direction of others. This is a major deficit in the building of democratic life. The experience of a managerial autocracy at work robs people of a sense of their own democratic agency. It contributes to a passive 'follow orders' mentality that sucks away the lifeblood of active citizenship.

It is just not realistic to expect active citizenship from people who have so little power to influence the rest of their lives. A lack of democratic engagement leads almost inevitably to a passive consumerist approach to democracy. This is reinforced by a political class that has grown adept at manipulating consumer preferences in the 'political marketplace'. This is done through a virtual industry that runs expensive campaigns and projects elaborately crafted images of honesty, sincerity and strength on the part of politicians. It is much easier to manipulate unreflective and insecure consumers of politics than it is to negotiate with a self-consciously activist citizenry. Consumerism in politics fits naturally into the consumer-oriented culture of 21st-century capitalism. When your main decisions revolve around choice of different cola and cigarette brands it is not a big jump to reduce democratic engagement to a choice between Brand X politician and Brand Y politician. If, however, you are used to having an active say in your workplace and community, this is unlikely to satisfy you.

Contested terrain

The history of the industrial workplace is also a history of struggle for control. In the earliest days of industrialism, factory owners worked hard to wrest control of production from artisans who had power through their skills and knowledge of the production process. With the rise of scientific management, inspired by the industrial engineer Frederick Taylor, work was divided into a series of easily timed repetitive tasks on an assembly line, the speed of which could be controlled by the factory manager. Ever since, workers and their organizations have been engaged in an ongoing struggle to bring some democracy to the workplace. This has often focused on the conditions of work – making sure that jobs are safe and done at a human pace with adequate breaks. These struggles, to which many trade unions have committed themselves, deal with more than money issues and move 'beyond the fringe benefits'. They have also concentrated on the length of time spent working. The struggle for the 8-hour day has now been replaced by a movement for the 30- or 32-hour week. The idea is that work should not dominate life in the way that it has through most of the history of industrial capitalism.

It is a natural progression for workers and their unions to start demanding a say over investment decisions – over what is done with profits. Should these go to stock dividends and CEO (boss) bonuses or be plowed back into the business to strengthen it? The point of entry for this kind of democratic demand

---

Strong democracy: many faces of workplace democracy

Experiments in workplace democracy in the industrial North vary from small community-owned bakeries and artisan shops to entire industrial enterprises taken over by their workers – often as an alternative to bankruptcy. In the poor countries of the non-Western world self-organized enterprises are often the only alternative in the absence of private investors willing to undertake the risks and low profitability involved. While such endeavors come and go, they together mark a persistent effort by people to control their own economic fate and provide the seeds of a future democratic economy. Here are just a few examples:

- In 1956 the Mondragon network was founded in the Basque region of Spain by a Catholic priest, Don José Maria Arizmendi. This was the start of what has become one of the most significant experiments in workplace democracy in the modern world. The original worker-owned and managed factory, named ULGOR, numbered 24 members and manufactured kerosene stoves. Today, the Mondragon network includes over 86 production co-operatives, averaging several hundred employees each. It also includes 15 building co-operatives, several service co-operatives, seven agricultural co-operatives, a network of consumer co-operatives with 75,000 members and its own bank (Caja Laboral) with 132 branches. Mondragon has, over the years, come in for its share of criticism for its compromises with managerial efficiency and the realities of capitalist business competition. But while some of these criticisms may be valid, Mondragon is most frequently the issue of the right of capital to dispose of 'surplus' workers by simply laying them off. Such issues are sharpened in times of severe economic contraction such as the 2008/09 credit crunch. In such conditions, workers are prone to be aggressive in demanding a greater say over the workplace. Amid the economic collapse in Argentina that started in 2001, workers took over some 150 enterprises, including hotels, glassworks and confectionery firms, many of which are still going. This may provide a model for workers elsewhere whose companies are faced with bankruptcy.

European unions in particular have tried to influence not only *how* things are produced but *what*

---

remains one of the few large-scale efforts at co-operative industrial organization and, as such, has many lessons to teach.

- In five dusty Mayan villages on the Yucatán Peninsula in southern Mexico is the Chac Lol Co-operative. Chac Lol (which is Mayan for 'red flower') produces corn tortillas. It runs five tortillerias that provide hot food for villagers. The co-op also runs several stores, a livestock farm of sheep and goats and a shoemaking enterprise. The highest authority in the co-op is the General Assembly, where all members get to vote. The structure is modeled on the Mondragon co-ops (see above). The co-op provides a living wage for those who work there, as well as economic and political independence from the PRI party, which until recently had ruled Mexico for decades. According to Ester, one of the cooperativistas of Chac Lol, the co-op is an instrument of liberation providing a way for them to be owners of their own means of production. It offers better working conditions and a higher standard of living, particularly for women.
- In Japan, older workers are starting to form worker-run companies in the face of the collapse of the country's lifetime employment system. Older workers who are laid off find it particularly difficult to find new jobs. One such company, The Building Service Engineering Group, is made up of 70 worker-members, whose average age is 66 years. This worker co-op, made up of ex-electricians and boilermakers, provides a building maintenance service and has proved very profitable. Most older worker co-ops focus not on profits but on providing stable employment under flexible conditions, geared to the special needs of older workers so that they may lead well-rounded lives.

is produced. The trade union movement has long been on the record for its opposition to military hardware and more recently in favor of ecologically benign products – public transit rather than private cars. The Australian trade union movement has battled against uranium mining and for green bans of construction projects that lead to a deleterious quality of urban life. On the level of governmental action, labor has traditionally called for intervention to limit owner/ manager sovereignty over the workplace and to give broader guidance to investment and production decisions. Such demands are in direct violation of the rights of property that are at the center of the strong market/weak democracy model. To be truly effective, however, they must pull workers into action as citizens beyond what can be bargained for at the level of individual enterprises.

Strange bedfellows

Capitalism and democracy have from the beginning been uneasy bedfellows. Most definitions of democracy imply a certain level of equality. Many of the original democratic theorists, Jean-Jacques Rousseau and Thomas Jefferson, for example, imagined democracy would be based on a republic of more-or-less equal smallholders where economic equality was not a major issue. They never had to conceive of how it might work in a society with a small minority of wealthy investors and employers and a vast class of non-owners and employees.

Unequal citizens have unequal resources (money, time, education, inclination) to bring into the arena of democratic decision-making. If Microsoft's Bill Gates is worth $50 billion or so, he can buy a lot of 'democracy'. In these circumstances democracy is eroded. The best of democratic theory assumes that some basic equality is necessary if citizens are going to exercise a more-or-less equal weight in shaping the direction of political life. Capitalism, on the other hand, with its ethos of 'possessive individualism', values above all the right to acquire as much property and wealth as possible. This is considered a just reward for an individual who exercises skill, ingenuity and initiative. The wealth and property thus acquired can be passed onto the next generation who may or may not be skillful and ingenious. Under capitalism, inheritance has gradually created a class of wealthy people who control the productive resources of society (factories, real estate, capital, access to raw materials and credit).

This inherited advantage is today largely what dictates the life chances of most of us. While there is the occasional well-publicized 'rags to riches' story, most people realize that they have a better chance of winning the lottery than of rising into the economic élite by dint of their own effort. The willingness of people to accept such inequalities is mute evidence of a shoulder-shrugging acceptance of the power of wealth to shape supposedly democratic outcomes.

Capital's veto power

Those with inherited or any other kind of wealth are in a position of considerable advantage in being able to influence the 'democratic' direction of that society. This is done both directly and indirectly. The health of the economy (and the well-being of everyone) depends on the investment decisions of the people who control capital and wealth in modern times through powerful transnational corporations. They want 'a good business climate' if they are going to continue to invest. This usually means a profitable return on what is invested, a competitive labor market, political stability, freedom from expensive regulations (perhaps around work safety or environmental controls), and taxation levels which do not discourage investors from 'risking' their money. Where a 'good business climate' does not exist investors are likely to 'strike',

Democracy timeline

The table below depicts major events in ancient and modern history that have helped shape the development and spread of democracy.

1700s BCE	Hammurabi, king of Babylon, establishes the first legal code
212 CE	All freeborn citizens of Rome are granted citizenship by the Emperor Caracalla
221	The Han Dynasty in China includes official, but diverse news circulation
600	Book printing is invented in China
701	Japanese political law is codified
790	Golden period of Arabic learning
802	Germanic tribal laws are codified by order of Charlemagne
970s	The Fatimid Caliphate, Muslim rulers of the Maghreb and Levant, build al-Azhar University in Cairo, the world's first university
1119	Bologna University is founded in Italy; Paris University, in France, is founded in 1150
1215	England's King John seals Magna Carta – a charter proclaiming certain citizens' rights and accepting that the King is bound by law
c1440	Johannes Gutenberg invents the moveable-type printing press
1492	Christopher Columbus lands in the Caribbean (beginning European expansion)
1517	Martin Luther publishes his 95 theses, launching the Reformation
1619	The first representative colonial assembly takes place in America
1625	Hugo Grotius publishes *De Jure Belli ac Pacis*, which becomes the basis of international law
1646	The Treaty of Westphalia ends Europe's Thirty Years' War and ushers in the modern concept of the nation-state
1679	England's Habeas Corpus Act ensures no imprisonment without appearing in court
1689	The Act of Toleration and Bill of Rights is passed in England
18thC	The Age of Enlightenment begins in Europe
1762	Jean-Jacques Rousseau writes *The Social Contract*, which asserts that if a government fails to serve its subjects well, they should have the right to overthrow it
1775	Beginning of the American Revolution
1776	Adam Smith writes *The Wealth of Nations*
1776	The United States declares independence from Britain
1787	The American Constitution and Bill of Rights are established
1789	The French Revolution begins
1790s	A slave revolt in Haiti against French rule, led by Toussaint L'Ouverture, marks the first independence movement in Latin America
1800s	Apex of the Industrial Revolution
1816	Simón Bolivar defeats the Spanish in Venezuela; independence is confirmed in 1821
1829	The practice of *suttee* (widow burning) is made illegal in India
1833	Slavery is abolished in the British Empire
1848	Europe's 'Year of Revolution'
1859	John Stuart Mill publishes *On Liberty*

1885	The Congress of Berlin initiates the 'Scramble for Africa' by major European powers
1885	The Indian National Congress is founded, beginning the campaign for home rule
1893	New Zealand becomes the first nation fully to establish a system of universal suffrage (including women)
1917	Russia's Tsar is deposed by two revolutions
1918-39	Women win the vote in much of the Western world; mass political parties emerge in Europe
1919	The League of Nations is founded
1924	The death of Lenin leaves Josef Stalin in control of the Soviet Union
1925	Benito Mussolini becomes dictator in Italy
1933	Adolf Hitler comes to power in Germany
1944	The first free presidential elections take place in Guatemala
1945	The defeat of the Axis Powers ushers in the process of democratization in Europe and Japan; the United Nations is established
1947	India and Pakistan gain their independence
1948	The Marshall Plan helps rebuild war-torn Europe; The UN approves the Universal Declaration of Human Rights, guaranteeing all people in all countries their basic rights
1951	Libya declares its independence (beginning the post-war decolonization of Africa)
1956	Hungarians rebel against Soviet power but are suppressed
1964	The US Civil Rights Act bans racial discrimination in federal funding and employment
1968	Czechoslovaks rebel against Soviet power in The Prague Spring but are suppressed
1972	The US Congress passes the Equal Opportunity Act in response to the growing women's movement
1980s	Latin America's military dictatorships tumble one by one
1987	Mikhail Gorbachev introduces *glasnost*, or 'openness' – a loosening of Soviet Communism
1989	Fall of the Berlin Wall; Popular pro-democracy protests take place in Beijing's Tiananmen Square but are crushed by the Chinese Government
1991	The Soviet Union disintegrates as the Communist Party loses power; democratic elections are held in Russia and throughout Eastern Europe
1994	The African National Congress wins the first free universal election in South Africa.
1990s	Use of the internet becomes widespread; Many African countries that were previously one-party states hold democratic elections
2002	The International Criminal Court is established to prosecute individuals for genocide, crimes against humanity and war crimes; After a long independence struggle, Timor Leste becomes the first new sovereign state of the 21st century; The African Union is founded
2006	Evo Morales becomes President of Bolivia – the continent's first indigenous leader
2008	Barack Obama is inaugurated as the first black US President

which could bring on a recession or even contribute to a depression. When the socialist government of François Mitterrand was elected in France in the early 1980s with promises of egalitarian reform, investment dropped right off. It went from the annual 4.4 per cent rate France had experienced from 1965 to 1980 to -1.21 per cent in the first three years of the socialist government.[1]

Other investor strategies may involve transferring their investments from less to more profitable sectors of the economy (say from steel to computers) or to transfer their investments to another part of the globe entirely to take advantage of a better business climate or 'lower wage jurisdiction' in, say, Bangladesh or the free trade zones of Mexico. It is obviously easier for some businesses (such as textiles or electronics assembly) to take advantage by shifting to a more favorable investment regime than it is for others. Levi Strauss, the original manufacturer of blue jeans, has, for example, laid off almost 30,000 largely unionized workers in the process of shifting its garment factories to the low-wage Global South.[2] Barack Obama's plans for US healthcare reform may be endangered by capital flight from the privatized US health sector.

Occasionally an investor strike is not just an economic reflex but an overt political act, as in Chile in the early 1970s when the international and Chilean business communities conspired to create conditions of political instability, laying the groundwork for the overthrow of the democratic government of Salvador Allende by the military. Such overtly political 'investment strikes' are rare and usually unnecessary as most politicians are compliant and understand the rules of the game. More frequent are investment strikes that affect just one sector of an economy – for example, the construction of rental housing, because of too strict rent controls; or investment in oil and gas exploration because of high royalties or taxes at the pump. The ability of major industries to run a kind of 'investors' auction' to see which jurisdiction (municipality, province, national state) comes up with the best package of pro-corporate policies severely restricts the right of communities to decide policy for themselves.

Debt squeeze

Another indirect way capital limits democratic possibilities is through the public debt held by nearly all nation-states and local governments. The political class is very nervous about offending those who hold the strings of debt – the major private banks, the International Monetary Fund (IMF), The World Bank and so on. A bad report from the IMF or a revision of a credit rating by a big New York bond-rating agency like Salomon Brothers or Goldman Sachs can bring on a credit squeeze and endanger economic equilibrium. Debt in the Global South has reached crippling proportions: the world's poorest countries pay almost $100 million every day to the rich world in repayments.

Large creditors generally do not like policies which mean payments to them are taking second place to public spending on healthcare or education, no matter how necessary these are or how popular with the electorate. This is one of the major reasons behind the policies of 'structural adjustment' that have so devastated the South. It is highly contradictory for the North to pontificate about the lack of democracy in the South while insisting on policies that are by their nature undemocratic and must often be enforced by the use of police-state tactics. Witness the riots and protest movements born of the frustration with IMF-inspired cutbacks, price increases and currency devaluations. There is perhaps no clearer contemporary example of how democracy and the 'free' market are fundamentally incompatible. There may be other roadblocks to democracy (a predatory military, a corrupt state élite, entrenched religious authorities) but ending the arbitrary external imposition of economic policy is a vital, if not necessarily sufficient, step toward democratization. Now, of course, the global credit collapse has books 'in the red' in both private and public sector almost everywhere. Still, major financial institutions seem to have a lot more clout setting out the terms of their own bailout than even quite large governments in the Global South.

Paying the piper

The other way the wealthy influence the direction of democratic decision-making is through the use of money to ensure favorable results. This direct consequence of 'some being more equal than others' is more visible and thus more controversial than the indirect veto (although perhaps not as effective), as many see it as a question of simply 'buying' democracy. Yet this is also quite complex and works itself out in myriad ways. Those with money can contribute to politicians and parties (usually but not always conservative ones) so they can run more visible and effective campaigns. More money means more ads on TV and everywhere else. More money means a more effective campaign machine, more highly paid pollsters, more tele-canvassing, more focus groups, more lavish rallies, the best professional designers, consultants and spin doctors. The list is almost endless, and given that the last US presidential election is estimated to have cost the candidates more than a billion dollars, it is growing longer all the time. The corrupting influence of money on campaigns is somewhat alleviated in those places with stricter spending controls and limits than the US but it still plays a large role almost everywhere. And, as US political consultants spread their vision and their skills to 'export' markets, such controls are coming under increased pressure.

Once politicians do get elected, those who can afford to pay well-connected lobbyists to influence the complex legislative process are 'more equal' than everyone else who just sits in front of the TV and wonders where all that new spending on healthcare or those tougher environmental regulations have disappeared to.

In most cases we are not talking anything as crude as direct bribery – although, as organizations like Transparency International continue to show, this remains a serious problem in the sphere of the former Soviet Union and much of the non-industrial South. In China it is estimated that as much as eight per cent of the Gross National Product goes from foreign capitalists to the families of the ruling Party bureaucracy, allowing them to set up and operate in the newly liberalized economy. China is, of course, not a democracy, but a similar process of buying officials and politicians is widely held to go on in India over the rewarding of defense contracts. Bribes in the democracies of the industrial world have more to do with job opportunities once you leave office.

But usually the process is an altogether more subtle one. It is a question of showing legislators sensible and realistic compromises that do not step on corporate toes. Watering down this piece of legislation. Pushing for voluntary compliance rather than direct enforcement of work or consumer safety and environmental standards. Pointing out how 'out of step' regulation or other public intervention is compared with what is happening in other more market-friendly jurisdictions.

Shaping the debate

Another corporate 'more equal than others' effect on the democratic agenda is achieved by using their resources to shape public debates. Hundreds of millions of dollars are spent every year to hire expensive public relations companies such as Ogilvy Worldwide, Burson-Marsteller and Hill & Knowlton, who are expert at finding the best way to put out the corporate message. The income growth of the PR industry was an astounding 263 per cent between 1978 and 1998.[3] Money is spent on advocacy ads to push for a decrease in capital gains taxes or to uphold the democratic right of tobacco companies to sell their products. Money can be used to cultivate journalists and other opinion-makers. To 'greenwash' the behavior of oil and mining companies, environmental education kits can be offered free of charge to cash-strapped educational institutions. Corporate names and logos pop up almost everywhere, from product placement in the movies or on TV, to corporate dedications that appear on sports stadiums or your local public library. The ubiquitous Nike swoosh is the classic example. With the public realm squeezed of resources, don't be surprised if your local library gets named after the McDonald's hamburger chain. The corporate message amplified by the liberal use of cash is by far the loudest to be heard in the democratic arena.

Welfare capitalism

The major effort to reconcile unbridled capitalism with democratic values has been through the evolution of an extensive regulatory and welfare state. The welfare state restored a modicum of balance between the demands of capital for profitable investment opportunities and the needs of everyone else. Starting in the Great Depression and picking up speed at the time of World War Two and after, this hybrid government attempted to ameliorate the worst inequalities of the system and prevent corporate abuse of the citizenry. Gradually a kind of consensus started to take shape that didn't much interfere with corporate domination of the economy but counterbalanced corporate power in the more general public interest. Such policies oversaw unprecedented growth based on the notion that government spending and national employment policies could counter or at least dampen the boom-and-bust business cycle. With the march to power of the New Right in the 1980s, this consensus came under heavy attack. A Keynesian program and the idea of government implementing a national economic strategy were replaced. An agenda of deregulation, cuts in social entitlements and reduction of the public sector swept across almost all borders. Democratic attempts to counterbalance the inequities of the market went into freefall. With the intensification of globalization in the 1990s and accompanying draconian policies of market-oriented structural adjustment in the Global South, inequities of wealth reached levels not seen since the days of robber-baron capitalism in the late 1890s. It is perhaps not surprising that the period from the 1890s up until World War One can be identified as the first great wave of corporate-led globalization. The accompanying inequities of power (then and now) have succeeded in stunting the democratic promise.

Through myriad ways, both direct and indirect, the rampant inequality in both economy and society is poisoning whatever democracy we have left. The underpinnings of a formal political democracy are constantly undermined by inequality. Its increase over the last couple of decades in the context of a global economic life dominated by a couple of hundred major transnational corporations and banks bodes poorly for our democratic future. These corporations are constantly gobbling each other up (Chemical Bank and Chase Manhattan, Bank of America and Security Pacific) creating fewer and fewer players at the top. They now dominate some two-thirds of global trade. In straight economic terms, the major corporate players outweigh an increasingly large number of sovereign states.

The perceptive social critic Christopher Lasch points out the near impossibility of limiting the distorting impact of wealth on democratic outcomes. He believes that 'the difficulty of limiting the influence of wealth suggests that wealth itself needs to be limited. When money talks, everyone else is condemned to listen. For that reason a democratic society cannot allow unlimited accumulation.'[4] It is quickly becoming a question of either democratizing the economy or having a despotic economy sweep away the last vestiges of meaningful political democracy. While no one is about to take away your right to vote, whether or not you exercise that right will matter less and less.

The ideological sleight of hand used to reconcile market domination with political democracy is the notion that connects unimpeded market activity with an economic freedom. This is then taken to be the basis of political freedom. This was indeed a powerful argument when it juxtaposed itself to the economic inefficiencies and shortages of the despotic state socialism of the Soviet sphere. It even had some resonance for critics of corrupt state bureaucracies in the Global South and those who decry the arbitrary nature of welfare state bureaucracies in the North. But today most of this is history: even the authoritarian socialism of China and Vietnam is adapting itself to the market as the main tool for organizing economic life. They have been very successful in doing this – particularly China, which has experienced phenomenal economic growth while maintaining the despotic rule of the Party. This is proof (if any were still needed after the sordid history of corporate partnerships with the various military dictatorships of the South) that the economic freedom of the market is perfectly compatible with a lack of any basic democratic rights in the political sphere. This severely undermines the case of the 'free market' liberal economic and political analysis. Today's icons of this 17th-century truth – the whole edifice of well-funded New Right thinking inspired by the neoliberal economic philosophers

Friedrich von Hayek and Milton Friedman – are hard pressed to explain these new forms of market despotism. Combine this with the collapse of people's livelihoods in 2008/09 (unless you were getting executive bonuses) and the case for democratic market stability is weak indeed.

Economic freedom or economic democracy

It is a major misnomer to refer to 21st-century global capitalism as an example of economic freedom at all. This is a global economy dominated by a few hundred major transnational corporations and banks which control the fates of not only the tens of thousands who work for them but also most of the world's nation-states who must compete for their favors. Most are dwarfed and thus intimidated by their economic might. Economic freedom in production belongs to those with access to capital and technology. Economic freedom in consumption belongs to a minority of the world's consumers who can afford access to the cornucopia of brand name products that are supposed to make up the good life. Even they must pay the price of the insecurity of living under a mountain of consumer debt. This liberal notion of economic freedom is a highly individual one whose only social dimension lies in the increasingly dim hope that the invisible hand of the market will harness private vice to create some distant overall public good. This is proving less and less defensible as social inequalities reach obscene proportions, the global ecosystem creaks under the weight of undirected market-led growth and the democratic promise is turned into a hollow shell.

Economic freedom and economic democracy are not the same thing. Economic democracy implies not a series of unimpeded individual and corporate rights but a collective process for controlling economic life. There is a vast amount of experience and theory involved in trying to do this. And while movements to democratize economic life have achieved only partial and limited results, this is largely due to an inhospitable context and the strength and determination of the foes of economic democracy – the corporate powerholders who dominate the world economy.

Debates between partisans of economic democracy tend to revolve around the role of the market. The core issue has to do with whether the market can be made to serve a democratized economy or whether it will inevitably undermine it.

It is possible to identify several tendencies in the ongoing struggle for an economic democracy:

State socialism
This was once the main alternative to market capitalism. Classic Marxist theory, modified by Lenin, held that central planning under a scientific élite working through the 'dictatorship of the proletariat' would reorder the economy in the interests of the broader society. This was the classic communist economy seen throughout eastern Europe, the former USSR and Asian communism. Although this highly centralized planning was helpful in the first phases of industrialization (at significant cost to both human and workers' rights), it quickly ran out of steam and major economic problems started to emerge. Shortages, corruption, gross inefficiencies and waste, and a chronically poor environmental record plagued state socialism. There was no effective feedback mechanism from below to indicate the economic wishes of society. Neither did its promise to democratize the economy amount to much as the bureaucrats in charge of production and planning ossified into a more-or-less permanent stratum. There was no real attempt to replace even the minimal feedback mechanisms of the market with more democratic forms that could articulate the desires of producers and consumers.

The regulatory state

In classic pluralist political theory this is the solution put forward to 'counter-balance' the weight of those who dominate the market. The idea is that the interests of society (to provide public goods such as health and transportation, protect consumers, workers and the environment, legislate inequalities, and so on) would be enforced by government. This state would be subject to influence by the whole range of opinion (environmentalists, unions, consumer groups), which would ensure an adequate level of regulation in order that market forces were channeled to meet a general public interest. But, as we have seen in practice, this is a contest of unequals, with the combined weight of the corporations with all their resources smothering alternative views and possibilities. Even the classic theorists of pluralism such as Robert Dahl have come to recognize that these power inequalities threaten the foundations of democratic contestation. The regulatory state has also adopted a very hierarchical top-down style which has alienated public opinion. There has been little consistent effort to democratize government and involve an active citizenry in helping to police inequitable and unecological market outcomes. To make matters worse, this popular hostility to an arbitrary and bureaucratic state has been seized on and amplified by conservative politicians. The resulting neoliberal offensive has been used to help roll back government, increasing inequalities and putting the environment and public health in jeopardy.

Market socialism

This theory is a modification of socialist doctrine brought about by left-wing economists such as Oskar Lange, W Brus and Alec Nove, reacting to the failures of state socialism's command economy. The case is most persuasively put forward in Nove's 1983 study *The Economics of Feasible Socialism.*[5]

Democratizing the economy

This basic adaptation of socialist theory holds that while most productive property (factories, natural resources, access to credit) should be either socialized or held co-operatively, the market remains the best way to decide things like prices, the flow of labor and most decisions to invest. Their idea is to combine the efficiency of the market with the democratization of productive units to ensure that no private monopolies can displace the public interest. Where investment decisions involve major externalities (effects on, say, the environment) a democratically accountable system of central planning would still have a role. Some sectors like health and education would be exempt from market-type criteria. The 'market socialists' envision a maximum of democratic consultation (they vary on the possibilities for workers' self-management) in factories and offices, thus overcoming the passivity of wage labor and enhancing active citizenship. There would need to be a continuing role for a regulating state to lay the ground rules of the economy, establishing broad agreement on incomes policy and taxes, and ensuring (in the absence of the corrupting influence of a corporate élite) that the market continues to serve the social goals.

Planning from below

Planning from below is a strategy for democratizing the economy more in line with the classic socialist vision. It foresees only a minor role for the market and puts the emphasis on a system of democratically controlled co-ordination of economic life. There are many versions of this, from radical visions of a highly decentralized society that has abolished money to elaborately thought-out systems for running advanced industrial economies. Some, such as the famous advocate of decentralization, EF Schumacher, and those he has influenced, see democratic control of investment and development at the local community level as the key.

The British political economist Pat Devine, in his *Democracy and Economic Planning*[6], puts forth a model based on what he calls 'negotiated coordination'. He details a system that would combine decentralization of decisions with the development of new democratic bodies like 'interest sections' and 'accountable planning commissions' at all levels of the economy. There would be workers' self-government in all enterprises. Planning advocates like Devine believe that market socialism relies too much on competing self-interests and will impede the emergence of a truly self-governing society and an economy that is organized around the democratically decided goals of human beings. Devine identifies the high level of management and administration that are already part of modern economies as an inevitable departure from a 'pure market'. He feels that if these were properly democratized they could act as the basis of a 'negotiated co-ordination' of an economy planned from below. He places a heavy emphasis on the achievement of equality and equal influence to create the capabilities necessary for a truly self-governing society.

The socialized market
This proposal for democratizing economic life is closely associated with the British economist Diane Elson.[7] She and other advocates of the 'socialized market' believe a strategy that bends market outcomes to social purposes will allow democratic intervention in a variety of ways that would ensure more popular control. Elson proposes a dramatic extension of common property rights over investment that would work through a system of participatory regulation to enforce social and ecological criteria on all major investment decisions. She believes that the seeds for this already exist in a range of corporate accountability initiatives that deal with such matters as minority

hiring, child labor, working conditions and environmental impacts. The 'socialized market' would include a basic income for all and reinforcing those markets (which Elson calls 'associative' and 'provisioning') would decentralize power and promote values of solidarity. Advocates of a socialized market believe that it is necessary to move beyond a sterile debate between 'market' and 'plan'. Elson concludes: 'My vision is not a "market" society but not a "bureaucratic" society either; it is a society in which democratically accountable state agencies structure markets so as to give a much greater chance for households and associations to flourish.'

The democratic economy debate

The debates over how best to democratize the economy tend to revolve around the differing weights given to planning and the market. While the 'socialized market' position represented above claims to transcend this debate, it does so only by looking at plan and market in different ways. It does not dispense with them. The key issue is whether or not market relations can be molded to reflect a broad range of interests or whether they inevitably serve those who are successful in achieving commanding monopolistic market power (as they do in a corporate-dominated economy). An auxiliary question has to do with whether market transactions will inevitably generate inequalities. And whether they can be made to take into account the use of natural resources and the impact of pollution.

Another issue revolves around whether the regulatory state can be made to reflect a consistent public interest, rather than unfairly reflecting the interests of those with market power as they do now. Advocates of 'democracy through planning' also have a number of serious issues to face. To what degree can planning of a highly complex economy be democratized? How can popular involvement and the technical expertise needed to run a modern economy be reconciled? How can a workforce and communities with little experience (or maybe even interest in) running an economy be given the confidence and motivation to do so? How can democratic institutions be developed to ensure a balance between the needs of consumers, producers and all the other interests (the environment, public health)? If the market is in danger of breeding inequalities, there is a danger that planning will degenerate into a top-down commandist approach. This would undermine popular participation and democratic possibilities.

These debates are fruitful and exciting. Their common starting point is that, without a thorough-going democratization of economic life, even the minimal level of political democracy we presently enjoy will be undermined. Democracy does not stand still. It is either extended or it retracts. It is clear that the present undemocratic organization of the economy inevitably undermines the equality needed to sustain a political democracy.

Nearly all advocates of economic democratization identify a role for workplace democracy as vital. The dictatorship that most experience at work saps democratic self-confidence in the population. Some economic democracy advocates fear that, with total self-management, workers would make the same narrow profit-seeking decisions as private corporations. They want to balance the power of self-managed economic units with that of consumers and others who could address the shortcomings of particular investment decisions. It is clear, however, that a much greater input from workers on investment and other production decisions, and self-governance of the rhythms and conditions of work (hours, shifts, holidays, pay, breaks, etc) are vital for any democratic economy.

Democratizing the economy

Disciplining democracy

C Douglas Lummis, in his excellent study *Radical Democracy*, draws a parallel between the role that the military used to play in limiting democracy and the role of the contemporary economy. It was the Prussian Wilhelm von Merchel who declared that 'the only remedy for democrats is soldiers'. And throughout the history of democratic struggle from Republican Rome to Pinochet's Chile, the bodies of democrats are piled very high indeed. But Lummis believes that the economy has now taken over the role of limiting democracy: 'Daily life is the economy, the very control system... captured in the ominous expression "business as usual"... democracy cannot be satisfied with a politics defined as a leisure activity driven out of the center of life (the economy) into occasional bits and pieces of "surplus". The democratic project will not be completed until it has succeeded in democratizing work.'[8]

A democratic economy requires a high degree of decentralization as a way of empowering local people and communities to control their economic destiny. For some this means a high-level of self-reliance (even autarky). Others see it as possible to combine decentralization with systems of equitable trade.

The various strategies for achieving economic democracy are not just pie in the sky. They can be seen in the co-operative sector at work in most economies. In the attempts to build fair trade between Northern consumers and Southern producers. In workers' struggles for more say on the job. In the various attempts to decentralize and democratize state socialism. In the democratic challenge to market-based investment criteria by movements to control workers' pension funds or other forms of ethical and socially responsible investing. All these efforts have a partial, slightly inadequate feel to them. They are not by and large part of an overall strategy to democratize economic life.

And such attempts often feel like 'one step forward, two steps back' given the inhospitable climate in which they must struggle to survive. But they don't disappear. They keep popping up in a rich variety of forms. They are proof of the desire and indeed need for people to control their economic destiny – not just as atomized consumers and entrepreneurs but in a social and collective sense.

The present situation in our limited democracy is one where the political class that manages the economy takes the advice and is beholden to the interests of those who have managed to accumulate significant market power. A real democracy would be one where the tasks and priorities of economic management were based on the advice of, and beholden to the interests of, the broader society. Whatever the mixture of market, plan, socialized market, workers' self-management, decentralization, fair trade and ethical investment needed to achieve this must be worked out in practice and through creative experimentation. The exciting debate about what a democratic economy should look like can only stimulate this process. The fate of our current fragile and partial political democracy hangs in the balance. Only a thoroughgoing economic democracy will enable us to deepen and strengthen it.

Only in an economy beholden to the interests of the entire society can we hope to bring an end to what the French social theorist André Gorz calls the domination of economic reason. This kind of all-inclusive economic rationality, expressed through the under-regulated market, cancels out the possibility of an economics based on a thought-out human purpose. 'The market itself is not the goal of any of the actors that confront one another there; it is the space that results from their confrontation just as "traffic" is the result of all those who are driving their cars at any particular moment and have... an average speed imposed upon them by all the other drivers, none of whom has actually chosen it.'[9] At the moment this economic rationality (a rationality lacking reason in Gorz's view) is creating a world of compulsory labor that produces too much, uses up too many resources, distributes its rewards unfairly and is endangering the global ecosystem upon which we depend to survive. Only a viable economic democracy has a chance of redirecting economics to serve some sane human purpose – where people control capital, rather than its controlling us.

1 Samuel Bowles and Herbert Gintis, *Democracy and Capitalism*, Basic Books, New York 1987. **2** *New Internationalist* no 322, p 11. **3** O'Dwyer's Directory of Public Relations Firms, New York 1978 and 1998. **4** Christopher Lasch, *The Revolt of the Elites*, Norton 1995. **5** Alec Nove, *The Economics of Feasible Socialism*, George Allen and Unwin, New York 1983. **6** Pat Devine, *Democracy and Economic Planning*, Polity Press, Oxford 1988. **7** Diane Elson, 'Socializing Markets, not Market Socialism', *Socialist Register 2000*, Merlin Press, London 2000. **8** C Douglas Lummis, *Radical Democracy*, Cornell University Press, 1997. **9** André Gorz, *Critique of Economic Reason*, Verso, London 1989.

5 Beyond the nation-state

'The democratic idea itself is perhaps best thought of as a utopian aspiration... we need such aspirations if we are to resist the notion, made plausible by the seeming inevitability of globalization, that democracy, self-determination and the common good are ideas whose time is past.'

Steven Newman in
Globalization and Democracy.

Globalization and the politics of influence practiced by the major world powers is a constant limitation on popular sovereignty. It takes decisions out of the hands of elected officials or at least gives them the excuse not to act. This chapter evaluates the different efforts to move democracy beyond the nation-state – from structures of regional governance to the evolution of an international civil society and a cosmopolitan democracy.

DEMOCRACY IS USUALLY associated with the nation-state. The liberal democratic model of a weak democracy based on possessive individualism emerged in the 17th and 18th centuries not long after the nation-states of Europe and North America were themselves consolidated. While democracy does have broader, deeper meanings, its association as a system of rule within the context of national sovereignty leaves the nation-state as the main site of democracy (or the lack of it) in most people's understanding. We speak of whether a state is democratic or not. Or whether it has a good or bad record on democratic rights.

But sovereignty has always been limited in the international system of state relations that lie outside the control of even the most committed democrats. The difference between the United States or China and Gabon or Trinidad when it comes to the exercise of their respective national sovereignties is large indeed. Their capacity for maneuver to meet the needs of their citizens varies dramatically. If there is conflict between them it is never really a contest of equals. If, for example, there is a clash between the interests of a US-based oil company and an indigenous community in a remote corner of Ecuador, the capacity of the Ecuadorian Government to protect its citizens (assuming it even wants to) is limited by its overall relationship with the United States. The sordid history of gunboat diplomacy stretching across centuries – from Cortés in slaughtering the Aztecs in Mexico to US jets firing rockets that massacre Afghan villagers – is ample evidence that 'might makes right' is an enduring principle of international relations.

In ordinary times, it is usually more subtle diplomatic and economic influences that are used by the more powerful to get the less powerful to accede to their wishes. The speed-up of the pace of globalization and the rise of rules-based trade agreements enforced through the World Trade Organization and regional agreements like the proposed Free Trade Area of the Americas limit the sovereignty of nation-states, particularly on economic matters. In the last few decades there has been a 'downsizing' of the capacity of most nation-states to shape their own internal affairs, particularly in the realm of economics. The central thrust of globalization strips governments of their capacity to protect their own populations from the ravages of international competition. The economist Marjorie Cohen concludes that 'international trade agreements provide the impetus for the proliferation of minimalist states whose major function for the international regime will be to control their own people to ensure that they conform to the international trade rules.'[1] The globalization agenda has implicit in it a kind of 'downsized democracy' where democratic majorities can only protect the quality of their lives within the bounds set by a collection of corporate-inspired trade and investment rules. This has obvious implications for the kinds of democracy that are possible.

Overturning democracy

The kinds of policies that exist today in the industrial world (and significant parts of the South) came about through some kind of democratic process, no matter how imperfect. Change in such policies would usually require a public debate and often some kind of legislative act by an elected assembly of some sort. Cohen, echoing the views of an increasing number of critics of economic globalization, points out: 'Now, economic and political policy can be challenged through international trade law. These are laws that are interpreted and enforced by people on a plethora of international panels who are not elected and who do not have to respond to people, since individuals within a country have no access to them.'[2] In other words, many of the rules for ordering economic (and by implication political) life are set outside the democratic reach of most citizens.

This may not matter too much for those who are happy that the uncontrolled market is the best way to organize economic life. But for groups seeking more equality in everything from income distribution to regional development it is a very effective way of tying their hands. It also places significant obstacles in the path of those who value environmental integrity or worker health and safety over the profit-maximizing behavior on which the liberalization agenda is built.

The diminished power of the nation-state has become a major source of concern for political thinkers of all persuasions. For some, it provides a welcome stability and a useful economic discipline on wayward politicians. For others, it is a major violation of the democratic prerogatives of the citizenry from Bangkok to Berlin. But this is not just a matter of polite debate at learned conferences and in weighty academic journals. It has a real impact on people's lives and has provoked what may be the most profound democratic outbreak since the 1960s.

The anti-globalization movement

It started in the Global South and has spread rapidly, to the point where the architects of liberalization are now being challenged at every turn. Perhaps the first clear shot came back in October 1983 when half a million Indian farmers staged a day-long rally in Bangalore to protest at proposals for liberalizing agricultural production. Next it was the Zapatista revolt in Chiapas on 1 January 1994, which shook Mexico and brought into question the newly signed North American Free Trade Agreement (NAFTA). The Zapatistas called this treaty 'the death certificate of the indigenous people of Mexico'.

The democratic outbreak against trade liberalization spread like wildfire. Hundreds of street demonstrations and protests, petitions and conferences, food riots and campaigns followed in rapid succession. Networks of activists from both North and South shared tactics and strategic perspectives. Soon the whole trade liberalization program had become highly controversial. Revolt spread from the South to the North, culminating in massive demonstrations against the World Trade Organization in Seattle which resulted in a collapse of negotiations for a new global trade agreement. From Melbourne to Quebec City, street demonstrations and counter-conferences have become the norm, accompanying every major meeting that tries to advance the economic liberalization agenda. The common theme of this resistance is the belief that the liberalization agenda bypasses the democratic process. It disenfranchises citizens, taking away their democratic choices in order to conform to a regime of trade and investment rules designed to protect the prerogatives of transnational corporations. After the attacks on the US by Islamic fundamentalists in 2001, the anti-globalization movement started to ebb, morphing into an anti-war movement in opposition to the worldwide militarization and attack on democratic rights that was part of the Bush regime's 'war on terror'. But the economic meltdown and burst credit bubble show signs of re-igniting the movement that at any rate has been biding its time in the continued social summits held across the world every year.

Debate in the movement

A key debate amongst critics of this usurpation of democracy is over how best to deal with the globalization offensive. There are two positions emerging on the best way forward. One stresses the need for structures of democratic governance and an international civil society beyond the traditional nation-state. The other advocates the reassertion and possible enhancement of the traditional powers of the nation-state. It maintains that the nation-state is the proper site for democratic decisions to emerge. It holds that democratic arrangements are best organized and can only really work on a national basis. Advocates of this position generally feel that most multilateral institutions – everything from the International Monetary Fund to the United Nations or the International Court in the Hague – have an inbuilt tendency to be hijacked by powerful interests. Fortune 500 transnational corporations and banks or superpowers such as the United States are just better equipped to play the international game.

The evidence for this is clear enough. By and large, the institutions of global economic management have been consistently committed to what has come to

Free and unfree

Compiled by Freedom House, a US-based organization, this map breaks down the world of 2008 into free, partially free and unfree. This is a highly subjective judgment by an organization which is close to the US foreign policy establishment. For example, several left-leaning Latin American countries such as Venezuela, Paraguay and Bolivia are now considered only 'partially free', a status that they didn't hold in 2000. It is at least arguable that freedom from economic need (that you would find in Cuba for example) should also be part of Freedom House's criteria. Their judgments on most dictatorships are clear enough. Although using conventional measures of freedom they do, however, provide general orthodox criteria with which to agree or disagree. ■

be known as 'the Washington Consensus'. This is a fundamental belief that market relations should guide economic decision-making and that government intervention should be as much as possible discouraged. Public sector investment, subsidies to keep food prices down or to prop up small farmers, an industrial strategy designed to overcome regional disparities, an increase in the minimum wage: these are all policies that fly in the face of the Washington Consensus.

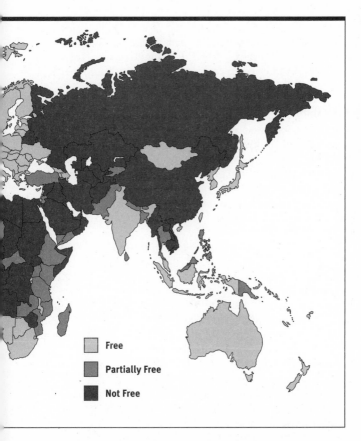

Free

Partially Free

Not Free

It matters little if they are wildly popular with the electorate. But already there are cracks in the Washington Consensus, as most of Latin America has abandoned it in favor of a social model more in keeping with the views of globalization's critics. The very policies of deregulation implied in the Washington Consensus resulted in the collapse of a severely overstretched speculative capitalism. A new terrain is emerging in the battle between those who want to save this supposedly 'free' global market and those who see its globalist face as an assault on popular democracy. While neoliberal globalization's reputation may be in tatters, its powers should not be underrated.

The United Nations
And it is not just the economic sphere in which the exercise of naked power politics takes place. The United Nations, which is supposed to rise above power politics and aspire to lofty international values, has been plagued by superpower domination. The world's most powerful nations (the US, Russia, China, France and the UK) hold seats as permanent members of the Security Council (with a veto on all resolutions) of the UN. As members of the Council they are able to exercise influence far beyond the weight of their respective populations. The Global South on the other hand is held in relative powerlessness throughout the UN system. During the Cold War the US had a particularly disdainful attitude towards the UN, regarding it as a 'bastion of the Third World and a center of socialist bombast'.[3] US politicians could always win brownie points at home by attacking UN waste and the supposed anti-Americanism (and fiscal waste) that held sway there. With the end of the Cold War however the UN became useful for successive US administrations bent on policing actions in various trouble spots around the world. The criteria for intervention had more to do with US strategic interests than with the amount of genocide or the number of refugees. Bosnia and Rwanda were allowed to burn but Kuwait and Iraq, with all that oil, were another matter entirely. The US uses the UN where possible but ignores it when necessary. When the UN refused to endorse an invasion and occupation of Iraq the US pulled together its so-called 'coalition of the willing' to do the job. According to John Bolton, George Bush's

man at the UN: 'When the United States leads the United Nations will follow. When it suits our interests to do so, we will do so. When it does not suit our interests, we will not.'[4] Hard to be blunter than that. The Obama Administration appears to offer greater respect for international opinion and multilateral institutions and endeavors. We will see.

Winner's justice

Even the International Court of Justice in The Hague stands accused (with some justice but also a lot of hypocrisy by those trying to divert attention from their own crimes) of dispensing 'winner's justice' on the question of war crimes. The case of President Bashir of Sudan (recently indicted for war crimes) is a case in point. He fulminates against Northern opinion as a cloak to cover his own culpability in Darfur. Still, the Court would never even consider whether those responsible for the decisions of aerial warfare (in Afghanistan for example) – no matter how high the 'collateral damage' (civilian death toll) – should be charged. So those advocates of democratic reform that are suspicious of attempts to build a counterweight in international institutions to balance both the arbitrary nation-state and the power of corporate globalization have ample evidence to back up their beliefs. The British political writer Timothy Brennan makes the case succinctly: 'We need to be very cautious in contemplating any cosmopolis that would short-circuit the existing nation-states in the name of the people: on that imaginary terrain too many powerful interests are already entrenched.' He believes that 'within a world system in which enormous disparities in national power persist, structures that give some chance to local or indigenous peoples to draw a boundary between what is theirs and what lies beyond, between what is open to the outside world and what is sheltered from it [are vital].'[5]

Beyond the nation-state

Brennan and other defenders of a revived national sovereignty believe that despite the overall record of nation-states being highly complicit in globalization, they still represent the single best hope for people to assert their democratic rights.

International problems

Most of the advocates of a cosmopolitan democracy (the term is from British political theorist David Held) recognize these obstacles to extending democracy.[6] They simply believe there is no choice. Part of their analysis

---

International civil society

Greenpeace, born on the Pacific shores of British Columbia, now monitors and supports struggles for environmental integrity worldwide from its international headquarters in Amsterdam. The Pesticides Action Network, a worldwide coalition of groups and individuals, exposes the dangers to food and foodworkers from the Philippines to Peru. The International Lesbian and Gay Association headquartered in Brussels links 350 groups in 70 countries engaged in the fight for the rights of sexual minorities.

These days it is not only nation-states and organizations representing nation-states (all the UN-related agencies) that operate in the international arena. Of course, for centuries business has also done so. Initially this was mostly merchant traders who would buy cheap and sell dear. Then it was finance capital. Gradually extractive industry and agribusiness became international. Manufacturing followed. Now transnational corporations dominate the global economy, controlling nearly two-thirds of global trade.

Since World War Two, however, non-commercial organizations have started to spread their wings beyond their borders of origin. Representatives of Amnesty International in Pakistan write letters to stop capital punishment in the US, while US members rally in support of Pakistani political prisoners. International organizations of writers like PEN International struggle to maintain the democratic space necessary for creative expression wherever threatened. International trade union organizations combine with student activists to expose sweatshop labor practices of the brand-name (the labor behind the label) clothing manufacturers from Central America to Cambodia. It's the same story with nurses, journalists, metal workers, lawyers and countless other groups. They are all finding it increasingly necessary to have an effective voice on the international stage.

comes from an abiding distrust of the democratic credentials of the nation-state. Where nation-states are democratic at all it is by and large a model of weak democracy with a political class well shielded from popular pressure that holds sway. The democratic inadequacy of the nation-state is further exacerbated by the increasing number of issues – refugees, toxic pollution, the arms trade, international financial speculation and illegal commerce, global warming, tax evasion, the debt burden of poor countries, a number of public health issues and shifting patterns of production

Development NGOs link together in 'international families' based on a rough similarity of approach – some fight for social justice and to end political poverty, others provide micro-credit or run foster parent schemes. Many feel the need to engage the major players of the global economy, whether Nestlé for marketing baby formula in unsuitable conditions in Africa or the World Bank funding mega-dams on the Mekong river. Approaches vary from polite lobbying, to pointed public criticism, to confrontation in the streets.

More and more of such organizations originate in the South. The Third World Network for example has offices in Asia, Africa and Latin America. It has become one of the main networks of the anti-globalization movement. Some are regional in focus: like TERRA (Towards Ecological and Regional Alliances) which brings together groups in Southeast Asia to stop the ecological carnage being visited upon the region in the name of development. Or the Asian Women's Human Rights Council that rallies the region around the negative effects of neo-liberal policies on women.

There are two major reasons for this explosion of democratic initiatives on the global stage. One is that many of the issues faced are international in both cause and potential solution. Everything from global warming to the trade in smuggled endangered tiger- and bear-parts demands action across borders if anything substantial is to change. Who can imagine trying to stop the international arms trade only from Manhattan?

The other stimulus for international grassroots actions is to act as a check on and a counterweight to the international actors in the global economy – the transnationals and the multilateral development institutions like the World Bank which facilitate their operation. If struggles against global powerholders such as the IMF and Nike were restricted by national boundaries, an already difficult battle would become impossible. ■

– that lie outside their borders. The cosmopolitan democrats have lent new cogency to the simple critique that the nation-state is 'too big for small problems, and too small for big problems'.

Even critics of the UN such as Phyllis Bennis don't think the world can do without it: 'However flawed the UN of the mid-1990s may be, the US should be pressed to support it financially and politically – not by reneging on billions in dues and destroying agencies that criticize or even diverge from the US position. The call from civil society should be one of championing the global organization – for the stark reason that there is nothing else to provide a multilateral voice for the majority of the world's countries – and sometimes, albeit rarely, for the world's people.'

Bennis sees the path of extending democracy into the international sphere as running right through the UN system: 'UN democracy means re-empowering the UN General Assembly, fighting for broader representation in the Security Council and less power for its veto-wielding permanent members. It means demanding that the UN reclaim its right to oversee – and overturn – the decisions of the Bretton Woods Organizations, so that global macro-economic policy is not set by the wealthy countries alone.'[7]

While Bennis looks to the UN, there are myriad other schemes for extending democracy beyond the nation-state, everything from traditional World Federalism to Pan-African and Pan-Arab ideas. There has been a rebirth of interest in Pan-Africanism in particular because of the poor fit between the colonial imposition of the nation-state form with that continent's rich diversity and geography. Africa has been plagued by secessionist movements, a poor record on minority rights, many border disputes and a strong tendency towards authoritarianism and military seizures of power. All have taken their toll on the poorest, most fragile part of the Global South. Small wonder there is a lively and growing interest in different political forms for African democracy. The new African Union is perhaps the first tentative interest in Pan-Africanist initiatives since the formation of the Organization of African Unity.

The European model

The most developed model of a regionalized democracy is that represented by European integration. Unlike other integration movements such as the Free Trade Area of the Americas (FTAA) and the Asia-Pacific Economic Conference (APEC), the Europeans have gone beyond economic liberalization to try and balance the economic with representative political institutions and extending the rights of the ordinary citizen. Europe has an elected parliament (elected by proportional representation) in Strasbourg with some important powers, continent-wide tribunals whose decisions on matters of human rights and the environment are more than merely advisory, mechanisms for dealing with cultural recognition and regional disparities, and a 'social charter' that at least begins to address questions of poverty and equality. European integration allows the free movement of labor while the FTAA and APEC are only concerned with the free movement of capital and commodities. Certainly it has not been all smooth sailing. There has been a tendency towards over-bureaucratization and corruption, particularly in the EU administrative headquarters in Brussels. The offices of corporate lobbyists dot the streets around the EU quarter. This has tarnished the young European experiment. And while the social rights enshrined in Europe are a start, they are not yet strong enough to counterbalance the powers accruing to transnational investors due to economic liberalization.

Still, the new Europe remains the best hope for nationalities and regions sitting uncomfortably within existing nation-states – the Catalans and Basques in Spain, the Bretons, Basques and Corsicans in France, the Scots, Irish and Welsh in the UK – for greater autonomy and self-determination.

Cosmopolitan democracy

An ambitious scheme for extending democracy beyond the nation-state comes from the political theorist David Held. Held's 'cosmopolitan model of democracy' would extend accountability to the growing number of power centers and networks that now escape the jurisdiction of the nation-state in the globalizing economy. It is a layered approach that involves deliberative institutions at all levels and a renewal of citizen participation as a badly needed tonic for democratic political culture. Held sees an international civil society as one starting point and impetus for this. He puts heavy emphasis on a further development and enforcement of international law and regulation to rein in the arbitrary use of extranational power. He calls for a principle of self-determination at all levels with representative and deliberative bodies globally, regionally, nationally and locally. He clearly sees economic regulation with the goal of greater equality-based outcomes as a central principle. This is a clear departure from the economic liberalization agenda of 'leaving it all up to the market'. Some such initiatives are already under way as the ATTAC movement tries to bring in an international tax on currency speculation. Others are formulating a 'bit' tax on the profits of international telecommunications that escape 'capture' by national tax authorities.

Held knows such proposals are ambitious and will not come easily. 'While the circumstances are clearly fraught with danger, and the risk of an intensification of a sectarian politics, they also present a new possibility: the recovery of an intensive and participatory democracy at local levels as a complement to the deliberative and representative assemblies of the wider global order. That is, they contain the possibility of a political order of democratic associations, workplaces and cities as well as nations, regions and global networks.'[8] So Held stands on the ground of extending democracy simultaneously both downwards to the local and upwards to the global. Such a visionary proposal would end the monopoly of the nation-state as the sole significant site for democratic deliberation.

Whatever the merits of either a reinvigorated nation-state or the extension of democracy into the international sphere, the problem of unaccountable global power has to be addressed. For the future of democracy is starting to look pretty grim. Our weak-willed political class perched in isolated nation-states and blinded by a globalist vision of a brave new world is simply no match for the large corporations and the international bureaucracies that are facilitating that vision. This political class has proved all too willing to join a 'race to the bottom' (in environmental standards, wages, social programs, the quality of life) in order to compete for trade and investment capital. It seems to matter little to them what their various electorates actually want and need.

The nation-state advocates are accused of standing for a dubious nostalgia that history has already passed by. Those who advocate an internationalizing of democracy are accused of abandoning its best defense with a wild jump into the future that is at bottom a kind of capitulation to corporate globalization. This polarization is probably not useful. It seems likely that some kind of hybrid strategy that affirms people's right to decide on all levels needs to emerge from this debate. It makes little sense to fight for strong democracy only or mainly on one level. The energy and imagination of the anti-globalization movement faces a multilevel world of power, with the central axis of the whole system running through Washington and New York. It needs a multi-pronged process of democratic action that entrenches popular power in local communities and regions but also projects it onto the national and international stage.

1 'Women, democracy and the future of nations', Marjorie Cohen in *States Against Markets*, eds Boyer and Drache, Routledge, London 1996. **2** Cohen, op cit. **3** *Calling the Shots*, Phyllis Bennis, Olive Branch Press, New York 1996. **4** Bennis, op.cit. **5** 'Cosmopolitanism and Internationalism', Timothy Brennan, in *New Left Review* Jan/Feb 2001. **6** *Democracy and the Global Order*, David Held, Polity Press, Cambridge 1995. **7** Bennis, op cit. **8** Held, op cit.

6 Democratizing democracy

'The cure for the problems of democracy is more democracy.'

John Dewey, philosopher.

Popular discontent with our model of weak democracy has undercut confidence not just in those we elect but in government itself. This has rebounded to the benefit of those who would leave everything up to the market. Debate rages as to how to restore popular faith in democracy. This chapter looks at such issues as direct democracy, decentralization and greater proportionality that could breathe life into ossified democratic structures.

JOHN DEWEY, the renowned US pragmatist philosopher, did famous battle with Walter Lippmann, a notable champion of weak democracy. Dewey held out for a more profound democratic citizenship in which citizens were fully fledged democratic subjects who shaped the public realm. For Lippmann, democracy was all about technique and the arts of political manipulation. He helped shape the tactics of Woodrow Wilson who, after being elected US President on a pledge to keep the country out of World War One, reversed himself and dragged Americans into the slaughter of the trenches. 'Saying one thing and then doing the other' has since become almost the norm for the political class.

Dewey was appalled, but Lippmann placed himself on the side of those trying to 'manage' democracy. He concentrated on the 'arts of persuasion' and consensus-building, on technique and the details of exercising power.

It was a dispute that, by and large, it is safe to say Lippmann won in practice, whatever the merits of his case. Orthodox political science has become preoccupied with exit polls, interest groups, precinct-by-precinct voting and the mechanisms for exercising power. As the 20th century wore on, political theorists became preoccupied with the totalitarian enemies of democracy (fascism, communism, fundamentalism) and spent little time critically examining the democracy they were defending. In the 21st century, this is slowly changing as the theorists of democracy recognize the malaise that is starting to paralyze the system. It is heartening to see the wide diversity of ideas and programs to deepen democracy that is now starting to appear.

Direct democracy

Perhaps the purest form of democracy is the direct democracy that we inherited from the Athenian city-state. It is decidedly out of fashion today. For most of those who study and engage in politics, any notion of direct democracy is a dangerously utopian one that easily slides into demagoguery and populist intolerance.

But can we realistically expect active citizenship without at least some experience of direct democracy? Indeed, in the associations of civil society beyond the state – everything from the vendors' association in Kampala's central market, to the Girl Scouts of Indianapolis – ordinary people are engaged in making directly democratic decisions. They decide rules, define membership, vote on budgets, argue over policy. Literally millions of people around the world – everywhere from communist Cuba to free-market Switzerland – are thus engaged.

Without their participation it is scarcely possible to imagine how society would run at all. If it were left to a class of politicians directing a professional bureaucracy to run all social organizations, the inefficiencies and the cost would be unimaginable. Citizens also engage in direct action as a form of political participation. This is often the means chosen by the young and the marginalized, who have given up on the electoral opportunities provided by a weak representative

Strong democracy: letting people decide

Direct referenda have mostly been used to decide major constitutional issues. The number of such votes has increased dramatically in recent decades. The Danes decided not to join the common European currency. The Scots and the Welsh decided to have their own parliaments. The Quebecois decided not to leave Canada. The Chileans decided that they had had enough of military rule. Most eastern Europeans decided on the kind of post-communist political system they wanted. The New Zealanders decided how to change their voting system. The Spanish voted on a new constitution. In 2008 the Irish rejected the new European constitution, while in 2009 they accepted it. While some of these results overturned the recommendations of the political élite, most were soberly taken after thoughtful debate.

Only in a few countries – about half the US states, Italy and most prominently Switzerland – are referenda and voter initiatives used to consult the public on non-constitutional issues. Referenda are usually organized from above by the government while citizen initiatives (such as anti-gun laws passed in some US eastern states) are initiated from below by groups of citizens and civil-society organizations. In Italy, initiatives backed by the Catholic Church that would have thrown out divorce and abortion were rejected by Italian voters. So was an automatic cost-of-living wage increase supported by the Communists.

These kind of initiatives are often supported by 'new groups' (feminists, environmentalists) or smaller political parties (Greens in Switzerland, the Radical Party in Italy) as a way of putting their issues before the public. Some concrete results have been electoral reform in Italy and a moratorium on nuclear power in Switzerland. Groups in the US have pushed for everything from tax reform to legalizing the medical use of marijuana.

Since the 1850s there have been nearly 500 national referenda in Switzerland. They are held on up to four days every year. Around three-quarters have been called by the government itself with the remaining quarter initiated from below. The number of such votes is on the increase.

The Swiss have voted on budget allocations, military spending, immigration policy, their relationship to Europe and countless other matters. Hundreds of other referenda and initiatives have taken place at the Swiss Canton (regional government) level, often about public expenditure, planning and development issues. The results are far from predictable but the politics of public choice is the main beneficiary. Switzerland, with a population of 6.5 million people, remains a relatively wealthy and conservative country. While the lack of economic democracy restricts the full development of Swiss political life, the direct forms of participation prove that letting the people decide is no pipe dream. ■

democracy. Their attempts to influence the course of events from the streets are often treated by the political class as unfortunate disruptions to orderly decision-making – or even as terrorist threats to the very idea of democracy. In fact new issues – environmental protection or minority rights – can often only enter the political arena through direct action and demonstrations. A complacent political class has at best a lukewarm interest in new issues and significant changes.

Restricted participation

Any meaningful direct democracy is, by and large, excluded from the political sphere. The reasons put forward for the impossibility of direct democracy sound a lot like the ideas that used to be marshaled against any democracy at all: 'The people are not educated enough, are too apathetic, too easily misled by demagogues, issues are too complex, the knowledge needed is too detailed and can only be grasped by experts, population size is too large, decisions need to be taken quickly and there is not enough time for lengthy democratic consultation.'

There is, of course, partial truth to some of this but it is also a failure of imagination and design. For one thing the current apathetic voter or non-voter can only be transformed and educated by actually participating. Under existing circumstances, the malaise discussed in Chapter 2 can only deepen. An interest in public affairs and a thirst for knowledge to inform thoughtful decisions will never come as long as decisions remain beyond the reach of the ordinary citizen. In politics, as elsewhere in life, learning comes with doing.

Experiments in direct democracy

Where elements of direct democracy have survived (some US states, Switzerland, a number of other localities that periodically allow their voters to speak directly), it is by no means clear that the quality of decisions is worse than if they had been taken by the political class. While there have been some unfortunate decisions, in such areas as taxation and immigrants' rights, there have been courageous ones on the medical use of marijuana and environmental protection. Direct democratic decision-making has proved in practice to be neither consistently reactionary nor colored by thoughtless populist reaction.

In some cases, such as the Canadian referendum on the Charlottetown Accords to revise the constitution in the early 1990s, voters rejected the view held by virtually the entire political class from Right to Left and turned down what they felt to be a threat to the capacity of the national government to enforce standards across the country. It is by no means clear that they were wrong about this. Politicians are often unpleasantly surprised when they try to use direct democracy as a mere tool of manipulation. A good example is the refusal of the Chilean people, once given the chance, to endorse General Pinochet's military dictatorship. If anything, initiatives of direct democracy have been marked by a healthy measure of thoughtfulness and even skepticism on the part of the public. Advocates in direct democracy contests are forced to address issues rather than engage in endlessly circular debates about the 'character' (usually manufactured) of particular politicians.

Greater direct democracy remains an important source of inspiration and ideas in the attempt to stiffen the backbone of a weak democracy where decisions are increasingly out of the hands of the majority. The political writer Ian Budge, whose pioneering work has helped revive interest in direct democracy, believes that it can be creatively combined with representative democracy. Budge thinks it possible to supplement out-of-touch parliaments and political parties with a regularized popular mandate where voters would endorse or reject significant policy proposals put

Strong democracy: can NGOs be democratic?

In the early 1970s Oxfam-Canada underwent a profound transformation. Inspired by an understanding of the political nature of what was then known as 'underdevelopment', a core group of Oxfam volunteers and staff fought an internal battle that altered the organization. The conventional top-down organization supporting apolitical 'gifts to the poor' no longer seemed appropriate. The changed Oxfam was something not very familiar in the non-governmental organization (NGO) world. Salaries were flattened so that everyone made the same money. The organization committed itself to a project of self-management – the shared responsibility of staff and volunteer activists. Radical decentralization meant much more power for regional boards and local committees across the country; much less in Ottawa. Power flowed very much from the bottom up. The external policy was shaped to link popular struggles in the South with those in the North; the understanding being that only a transformation of our own societies could significantly alter unequal power relations that shaped global inequalities.

To achieve this, Oxfam not only shifted its support towards popular movements in the Global South but also undertook to support popular education, poor and anti-racist organizations and challenges to corporate-led development in Canada. Over the years the organization devoted hundreds of thousands of donors' dollars to this work and did not shy away from the innovative task of public fundraising for these campaigns.

Such a bold shift in direction was not without its problems and discontents. The decision-making process for a radically decentralized national organization can be long and frustrating. No-one was ever willing to take someone else's word simply because of the position they held in the organization. Meetings dragged on. The public perception of the organization changed slowly. While core supporters were brought along, the mass influx of money and new supporters that came from disaster relief was harder to sustain.

The media still maintained the conventional view of Oxfam as a development charity and shaped public expectations in that direction. The role of a development NGO was, after all, to transform as many donors' dollars as possible to food in the mouths of hungry people tomorrow or at least the day after. Relations with government, including the Canadian International Development Agency, became strained and suspicious over everything from political engagement to bureaucratic reporting norms. Oxfam didn't shy away from controversial public statements. Oxfam-Canada was involved in a delicate and innovative balancing act to maintain its traditional charity functions while also taking on many of the characteristics of a social movement. To maintain its democratic ambitions, it had to sustain this balance and not fall off the beam in either direction.

Gradually the cobwebs of contradiction started to gather. There was a growing frustration of those in 'managerial' roles that their ability to manage was being hampered by too much democratic consultation and they were not being adequately rewarded for their professional credentials and responsibilities. Other staff pushed to unionize (to some degree in response), short-circuiting their own role as self-managers for that of militant workers. Money became short (due to a large degree to ill-thought-out investments in a trading company) and people started to look around for places to cut. The regional boards (too costly and time-wasting) and the domestic program (not a good fundraiser) were obvious targets. In those years many expensive consultants came and went and advice flowed freely.

Gradually Oxfam-Canada was forced back into a more conventional mold. Regionalization was abandoned in favor of a process of volunteer 'units' and 'unit assemblies' that meet so infrequently that any real policy input or oversight of the organization is difficult. Regional boards were dissolved. The numbers of volunteers were restricted to a few at the National Board level (who seldom discuss programs) and then those around the units. Volunteers who used to make up a vital part of program development and choices are now largely absent. Their role has been taken by professional staff. While many are still committed to support for popular movements in the Global South, there has been a cost. Cutbacks have largely wiped out the resources Oxfam-Canada used to provide to support popular education and social struggles in Canada. Staff in the regions and in charge of Oxfam's Canadian Program have been cut back while the Ottawa office has expanded. The 'professionalization' of the organization has been achieved at the cost of a vital internal democratic life. Many dedicated staff are still committed to the political goals set out by Oxfam but must now pursue them in the context of a professional development agency that has shed many of the characteristics of a democratic movement.

Oxfam-Canada now more closely resembles a conventional NGO model. But the context in which Oxfam operates has changed. Now the 1970s' analysis of 'political poverty' is widely shared amongst other NGOs and a growing anti-globalization movement in the country. The democratic experiment in Oxfam helped to shape this new context. The fate of Oxfam-Canada does, however, show how difficult it is to create 'democracy' in a situation of constantly swimming against the current. When expectations of the government, the casual donor, the media and an ideology of professionalism all run to the contrary, it is easy for the sources of democratic imagination to dry up. ■

forward by party-based governments. According to Budge, in this scenario 'parliament would change into an advisory, investigative and debating committee informing popular discussion and voting, rather than substituting for it.'[1] This could provide a popular check on the wild swings in policy and the influence of powerful extra-parliamentary groups on the professional political class. History might have been quite different if acts like the declaration of war or the imposition of widespread structural adjustment programs in the Global South could not have been implemented without first seeking a popular mandate.

Budge goes on to paint a picture of a reinvigorated and lively political culture under direct democracy: 'If a special organization were dedicated to ensuring fair electronic coverage of policy discussions, this could relay initial debate in parliament and possibly the proceedings of commissions of inquiry on the Swedish model; then go on to party broadcasts, deliberative discussion by representative samples and juries, transmission of local meetings, phone-ins, questions and comments to national media. In other words the whole gamut of current coverage should be systematically organized on a regular basis.'[2]

More thoughtful decisions

Critics claim that direct democracy would slow down the process of government. But this might just as easily be seen as a significant advantage. Policy decisions taken in haste are often regretted at leisure. Greater caution might temper the headlong rush towards an unthinking economic growth, trampling all obstacles and non-economic values in its path. The recent 'stimulus' packages that amount to giveaways to the rich and powerful are, for example, wildly unpopular with the public.

Direct democracy might also be a useful counterbalance to the egoism and self-enrichment of political leaders or the *raison d'état* so popular with the bureaucrats. Too often the prerogatives of the national security state are asserted as an automatic reflex to cut off more thoughtful debate. The extension of democracy to direct decision-making can be seen as a continuation of the decades of struggle to expand the franchise to all citizens. This bitter battle was won only after some very hard-fought campaigns from below. The struggle for a fair franchise was opposed with predictions of catastrophe, so we should not be surprised to hear such claims again. But on the evidence of a few US states and the Swiss example it would seem likely that popular mandate would have protected health and educational services better and done more for the environment. Budge and other advocates of increased direct democracy put great stock in the development of a network of interactive, new-technology-based media to facilitate broader-based democratic decisions.

This raises significant questions of access, ownership, cost and the potential manipulation of such media. But it also promises direct popular control without the bogey of endless boring meetings. Mass society can obviously not revert to a classical Athenian model of large town-hall type gatherings – although this method of local input could still play an important role in any decentralized political system. Neighborhood-type budget meetings in the communities of the Brazilian city of Porto Alegre have played a large part in creating a truly participatory municipal budget. In small towns, Majority World villages and urban neighborhoods this kind of decision-making could prove quite appropriate.

But whatever the method, the apathy and withdrawal of people from political life can only be overcome with meaningful participation and the growth of interactive technologies cannot but aid such a possibility. Already mass demonstrations like that against the World Trade Organization in Seattle and many other significant political movements have found a virtual meeting place on the worldwide web.

There is a modest but growing revival of interest in direct democracy. There are advocacy groups in many countries and biannual conventions of the Committee for Direct Democracy.[3] They are encouraged by the possibilities presented by interactive new technologies, in which they see the potential of a much greater amount of democratic deliberation and input. It is likely that the parts of the South (particularly rural areas) where there are indigenous traditions of popular decision-making could form the basis of a direct democracy there.

Limited representation

It is hard to imagine a working democracy that does not involve representative forms, whatever the mix with direct consultation of voters and popular initiatives from below. This opens up the question of what kind of 'representation'. The current system is one where we are represented in public political life by one or two sets of professional politicians – depending on whether we live under federal or unitary systems. These politicians are organized in 'more or less' democratic political parties. Such parties run the ideological spectrum from Right to Left (although differences between them are certainly narrowing). Some may represent particular regions or interests. The most successful have generally been the big brokerage parties – the Democrats and the Republicans in the US, the Liberal Democratic Party in Japan, the old Congress Party of India, the Liberal Party in Canada and until recently the PRI party in Mexico. Such parties have loose ideological commitments and use a vaguely populist rhetoric (often of the Left) while campaigning. They typically contain a number of powerful factions and interest groups, each of which stakes a claim on policy and economic rewards once the party is in power.

Parties of a more ideological stripe are gradually transforming themselves into this kind of 'brokerage' party in the depoliticized climate of market democracy (the transformation of Labour into 'New Labour' in Britain is a classic example). The kind of 'representation' one can hope to get from such parties (especially in situations where they monopolize power) is limited by the number of claims of other powerful stakeholders and by the extra-parliamentary corporate power embedded in the capitalist economy. The conditions under which a majority government governs have been variously described as 'an elective dictatorship' or, in British cultural critic Raymond Williams's telling phrase, 'the periodic election of a court'.

Williams traces the various notions of representation from the time of the Estates-General in revolutionary France, where representation was a function of social position, to our notion that the elected 'represent' a geographic locality. While he grants a limited truth to such notions of representation, Williams goes on to champion 'an alternative idea of making present, in continuing and interactive ways, the various interests of those who are... represented.'[4] In other words, he envisages a regular system of accountability beyond the current arrangement of infrequent elections.

Under most present circumstances, our elected 'representatives' are only answerable to us in a very general sense. Once they have been elected, any number of factors may weigh more heavily with them than the wishes of their constituents – their own views, party discipline, personal ambition or the influence of powerful lobbies. By and large, voters do not get to hold them accountable until the next general election. In the meantime they form a virtual dictatorship – if they are part of a majority government. Even the meager exercise of the popular will implied by elections must overcome a multiplicity of unrepresentative forms (unelected houses like the British Lords or the Canadian Senate; religious councils like those which stymie the Iranian Parliament; the US Electoral College) that are designed to provide a buffer against unpredictable public opinion.

The very language of politics reveals how little 'representation' means in practice. Newly elected leaders often make the claim that they will put partisanship

Strong democracy: local self-government

Three times the council of the beautiful British Columbia foothill town of Rossland brought their salary increase before the 12,000-odd citizens of the town. Three times the citizens said no. Rossland is one of the few municipalities where the citizens have this power. Inspired by municipal administrator Andre Carrel, Rossland in 1990 passed its own municipal constitution bylaw, which allows for a system of referendum and citizens' initiative.

The idea was simple and revolutionary. 'All bylaws should be subject to citizens' consent, implied or expressed, at the discretion of citizens themselves, not only where the law (or council) deemed it appropriate.' In other words the citizens in Rossland were engaged in the profoundest expression of strong democracy – self-rule.

The people of Rossland used their new powers to push through dramatic improvements in water quality, approving Can$4 million (US$2.5m) to establish British Columbia's largest slow sand water filtration and first ozone water disinfection plant. It established a Water Quality Reserve based on a new property tax. Drinking water quality has become a major issue in Canada since the poisoning of over a thousand citizens of Walkerton, Ontario, due to irresponsible provincial downloading and privatization. The people of Rossland also took fire and recreational facilities back under municipal control in order to control expenditure and program quality.

There was none of the generalized tax-slashing and program-gutting that critics of direct democracy so feared. Carrel reports that attitudes towards local government have undergone a profound shift in Rossland. 'The damned government' excuse has lost much of its credibility, because municipal policy decisions are either approved directly by a majority of the citizenry through referenda, or they are consented to by their abstention. Governing under the umbrella of a municipal constitution, citizens have defined the policy fence within which their council may govern their municipality.

This sounds good but it is all illegal. Canadian towns and cities do not have the power to govern themselves, either directly or indirectly. Like most municipalities in other parts of the world, Canadian local behind them and will from now on set themselves the task of representing 'all the people'. This is, of course, ridiculous and insulting to those who worked against them in the election and are absolutely opposed to their program. It is also insulting to those who believe in their program and supported them in the election.

This remains a source of irritation for those who

government is simply a creation of those levels of government (in the Canadian case provinces) immediately above them. The 1986 disbandment of London's Greater London Council by the Thatcher Government in the UK provided graphic evidence of the colonial status of municipal government there. Canadian provincial governments can and have dissolved municipalities, altered their taxing powers, changed their boundaries, reduced the number of elected representatives they can have and downloaded service responsibilities from higher levels of government. Most Canadian major cities have either undergone or are undergoing a brutal process of amalgamation with their suburbs, whether they want it or not. In Canada's largest city, Toronto, over 70 per cent of the electorate voted against amalgamation in a referendum but it was imposed by the Conservative provincial government anyway.

The subordinate status of local government is a severe impediment to true democracy. Andre Carrel believes that the colonial status of municipalities needs to be challenged if democracy is not going to continue to deteriorate into a mass of disgruntled consumers rather than citizens. The 'one size fits all' municipal policies of higher levels of government deny the uniqueness of every municipality's problems and potential solutions. Carrel sees Rossland's experiment in direct democracy not so much as a blueprint that other places could copy but as a source of inspiration for doing things differently. A political contract between local government and its citizenry to seek not just consultation but also direct approval is very much a question of political will.

Carrel feels that the demands for directly democratic alternatives will only grow in the present context. He concludes: 'The idea of citizen empowerment is a powerful thing. As more governments strive to become "mean and lean", as public policy is increasingly determined by economic policy and as economic policy is increasingly shaped in global terms, interest in meaningful citizen participation in decisions that will alter the community will grow.' This places the fight for municipal self-governance directly in the path of the steamroller of globalization. ∎

Taken from Andre Carrel, *Citizens' Hall: making local democracy work*, Between the Lines 2001.

Democratizing democracy

hold to democratic principles on both Left and Right. The former see the inequalities in the rest of society biasing representation towards the already powerful, while the latter see a bureaucratic state remote from the control of the ordinary citizen. Certainly more direct democracy would act as a popular check. A plethora of ideas for greater empowerment of and participation by ordinary citizens just won't go away. These take a variety of forms. Referenda over key questions, recall of individual representatives or entire governments, variations on the voting system, decentralization, town hall meetings, term limits to prevent a political class from entrenching itself, federalism, deliberative democracy involving citizen juries – the list for revitalizing democracy is almost endless. The thread that runs through all such proposals is putting the people back in the democratic picture.

The proportionality debate

The actual electoral system plays a big role in determining how well citizens feel represented. Unlike systems of proportional representation (PR) where it is easier to express minority views, the 'first-past-the post' (FPTP) system tends to produce two or at the most three largish 'consensus' political parties grouped around the Center-Left or the Center-Right. It is a situation in which the brokerage parties described above flourish. Countries currently using FPTP include India, Canada, the US, the UK and, with some variation, France. It is exceptionally hard for new parties with different ideas (a Green Party for example) to break through the political monopoly of FPTP. In the FPTP system if I vote for a candidate whom I know will not win in my riding or constituency, my vote is simply wasted. In systems based on proportionality all votes end up counting towards the final result and are not 'wasted'.

In most European electoral systems such votes are

tallied as part of the overall national result and help elect a group of MPs to parliament that express each voter's preference. This allows people to vote more with their 'conscience' and according to their desires rather than being put in a position of having to choose tactically the lesser of evils to ensure their votes will count. It is noteworthy that most of the systems of eastern Europe, and other societies like South Africa that have recently had the opportunity to shape new electoral systems, have chosen some form of proportional representation rather than FPTP systems.

The FPTP system is favored by the economic establishment and many political scientists because it trades democracy and minority views for political stability. There is often a conservative bias in favor of strong economic medicine and hard choices that a 'tough' leadership must take. This is, however, mixing up democratic principle with a desired policy outcome. The purpose of an electoral system is to 'represent' as accurately as possible the wishes of the voters. The messy multi-party coalitions that are more typical of PR may not lend themselves to boss-type politicians like Margaret Thatcher or Ronald Reagan but they have consistently shown a higher degree of citizen involvement and interest.

Just a few statistics will give a sense of the bias built into FPTP. In national elections under FPTP systems, hundreds of thousands of Green voters in the US, Britain, Canada and elsewhere get no representation at all, despite the numbers of their votes. In 2005 Britain's Labour Party retained power despite the wishes of the 64.8 per cent of voters who cast their ballots for other parties.

FPTP has left a few very powerful and well-funded political parties – the Republicans and the Democrats in the US, the Labour and Conservative parties in the UK, Congress in India, the Liberal and Conservative parties in Canada – to dominate. Canada presents the classic case of a country both regionally and politically balkanized by the first-past-the-post electoral system. Most political parties are under-represented in the House of Commons, with MPs drawn only from particular regions (although most have support across the country). The Liberal Party of Canada and the Conservative Party gain and retain power despite winning popular votes in the high thirties or low forties. Frustration among Canadians can be seen in the decreased membership of political parties and an increased refusal to vote at all.

Control from below

While proportionality in the electoral system may be part of the answer, it will not satisfy the requirements of a fully fledged democracy that values self-rule. Indeed, if a PR system is not modified by internal party democracy it will replicate many of the problems of the FPTP system, with élite negotiations between sectors of the political class far removed from popular control. Strains in the German and other Green parties (as they participate in government) are already starting to show up.

The requirements for a deepened democracy can be introduced through integrating elements of direct rule into the system. Other elements of democratic reform – term limits, citizen juries and assemblies, recall provisions – may also be useful. But unlike the basic formula of 'weak democracy/strong market' that the advocates of globalization are trying to install from Luanda to Liverpool, it is important to avoid a 'one size fits all' approach to democratic reform. There are sources of democratic strength in everything from the emerging civil society in autocratic China to indigenous consensual decision-making in Andean Latin America, as seen in Evo Morales' experiments in Bolivia. Democratic practice in a dense urban area (popular neighborhood assemblies and so on) is likely to be very different from democracy in a desert region of relatively sparse population. Each society must find strengths in its own traditions and shape a sense of 'representation' based on its own needs rather than simply importing the Western model of a weak democracy. This will involve active resistance to ideological pressures to adopt a US model as the only 'real' democracy.

In a variety of rich forms, however, the notion of who 'represents' us cries out to be broadened. Where we cannot 'represent' ourselves through direct voting on important policies or participation in local assemblies, we may still need to be represented. But this representation does not have to be by a few members of a more-or-less permanent political class operating from offices in some remote capital. Instead we need a rich variety of representation in our housing co-ops, workplaces, neighborhoods, schools and universities, regional planning boards or environmental advisory committees. This is the only way truly to democratize contemporary life. It implies a radical decentralization of power based on the principle that all decisions should be taken by those most directly concerned with them. A policy of maximum self-management could enrich and enliven, educate and animate democratic practice. Democracy would no longer feel like something remote, monopolized by a few 'all purpose' representatives, but part of everyday life where citizens had regular interactions with those charged with carrying out their wishes.

1 Ian Budge, *The New Challenge of Direct Democracy*, Polity Press, Cambridge 1996. 2 Ibid. 3 For a full list of direct democracy initiatives, see www.mathaba.net/www/dd/index.shtml 4 Raymond Williams, *The Year 2000*, Pantheon Books, New York 1983.

7 Democracy and ecology

'Find your place on the planet, dig in, and take responsibility from there.'

Gary Snyder, poet.

The environmental crisis is challenging orthodox democracy in some vital ways. A market democracy where real democratic power is traded for ever-expanding consumer prosperity is just not sustainable. The short time-frames within which most politicians operate cannot cope with the long-term impacts of ecological change. This chapter sorts through the toolkit of Green ideas for building an eco-democracy where environmental health is a first principle.

THE ENVIRONMENTAL DIMENSION is something relatively new for democratic thinkers to cope with. Classical democratic theory just assumed a bountiful nature where endless free goods were there for human enjoyment. They simply needed to be transformed into private property or were nature's free 'inputs' into the creation of commodities. But in today's world of collapsing ecosystems, shrinking resources and the widespread dispersal of toxins, the situation is very different.

Environmental issues have become a major focus of democratic action. John Locke or Jean-Jacques Rousseau could never have imagined the Chipko movement in the Himalayas trying to defend their forest resources and watersheds (and livelihood) against commercial logging interests. Nor could they have put themselves on the streets of Southern megacities like Mexico City and Bangkok where breathable air is at a premium. Environmental issues, if they existed at all, were local; the potentially catastrophic impact of unsustainable human activity on the global climate was simply unimaginable.

Whether it is endangered species and bioregions or desertification and the growing scarcity of usable water, environmental problems and issues amount to a major new challenge for democratic theory. How best to husband resources, minimize eco-impacts and slow a sustainable growth to manageable proportions presents a significant challenge to democracy. In the strong market/weak democracy model, the sovereign consumer is king – unless of course your income (or lack thereof) fails to translate into effective demand. The 'buy, buy, buy' ethos has a very strong hold on popular consciousness. It has the potential of pitting a consumerist majority on one side against a minority on the other who see the need to get off this unsustainable treadmill. Environmentalists are easily portrayed as people who want to 'spoil the party'. It is a classic challenge of minority/majority relations.

Short time-frames

Environmentalists also face the problem of the 'time-frame' of democratic politics as currently practiced. The politician must promise jobs and prosperity on a very short time-frame – with elections occurring every four or five years at most. Given our personality-based politics, with little substantive discussion of issues (on average, in the US a politician takes eight seconds to answer a question) the coinage of success in modern electoral campaigns often hangs on who promises to deliver 'the goods' most efficiently.

Although it is usually best to coat such practicalities as some kind of 'vision thing', it is really a kind of meat- and-potatoes politics. Questions of incremental climate change occurring over decades, the gradual extinction of plant and animal species or our obligation to leave future generations a livable world are difficult to turn into media soundbites. Politics as practiced makes it hard to turn such concerns into effective political programs. The fact that we are pushing a hundred species a day into evolutionary oblivion just never registers in the opinion polls. The difficulty in getting governments to agree to and meet even minimalist goals on climate change speaks volumes about the myopia built into the strong market/weak democracy model. Most politicians just don't see any votes in it. A more deliberative participatory democracy which engages people as citizens and not just as consumers would be no guarantee of better results, but it could hardly do worse. A slowed-down democracy, allowing more time for reflection and popular input, would afford more space than the frenetic 'silly season' of our current electoral campaign cycles.

Consumerism over citizenship

Eco-politics has tackled the question of democracy in a number of ways. Green political thinking tends to see contemporary society as suffering from a crisis of participation. According to this logic, citizens have withdrawn from public life and involvement and replaced these engagements with the pleasures of shopping and various passive entertainments. People have in a sense abdicated their role as citizens and make up for their powerlessness in the public arena through these compensatory activities – jet skis, all-terrain four-wheel-drive vehicles, computer paraphernalia and the latest designer clothing. It is hard to know what came first – the pleasures of consumerism or the powerlessness associated with the 'weak democracy' model. Most Green political philosophy puts at the center of its concerns a revival of popular participation and a trade-off between a richer quality of life (more power, less time working, a more democratic culture) against a reduction in the quantity of life (low-energy lifestyles and a reduction of conspicuous consumption). One form that participation could then take is to safeguard and renovate the natural world.

Tied to this notion of participation is a more-or-less radical advocacy of decentralization. Green political theory has a strain running through it that almost inevitably favors the decentralization of democratic decisions. The degree of decentralization is cause for heated debate within the various currents of Green thought. Some, like the fundamentalist factions that exist in most Green parties or the eco-anarchists and bioregionalists, believe that all society must revert to a simpler form and scale if we are to survive as a species. Their emphasis is then to create the forms of this new society that can live in harmony with their local ecosystem and defend it if necessary from corporate or other degradation. Eventually this would involve changing patterns of human settlement so that major urban conglomerations would be broken up. Democratic decision-making then would be a face-to-face matter, drawing inspiration often from the tradition of indigenous peoples.

Beyond the local

Other currents of eco-politics point to the fact that many of the environmental problems facing the earth are not solvable by operating simply on a local level. People in this frame feel that issues such as climate change, our somewhat besieged automobile culture and genetic engineering cannot be solved by concentrating power in local communities, no matter how democratically they are run. Furthermore, they hold that leaving the national and international arenas to powerful corporate and bureaucratic organizations would only mean that their decisions went unchallenged. Even so, they also believe in a notion of political democracy that decentralizes many decisions currently taken at the national level.

But other decisions involving planning, national standards for air and water quality, treaties to protect the environment and so forth, need to be taken at the level of regions, nation-states or even internationally. This strain of eco-politics calls for the democratization of these higher levels of politics. This is necessary not only to encourage broader participation and interest but to curb the unequal weight of those with a major stake in the current industrial system. Only then will there be a chance to restore ecological balance and healthier lives.

Southern complexities

In the Global South the matter is even more complicated. Ecological sentiment is often held as coming from a position of Northern privilege. While this is slowly changing as Southern environmental movements grow in strength, it is still a widely held perception. It has not been helped by the cavalier attitude of some Northern environmentalists to the life-and-death situations many people in the South face every day. But in a situation of real (as opposed to manipulated) economic scarcity there is heavy pressure on limited resources. Poverty and the threat to actual survival can force those at the bottom into a desperate misuse of resources (seen in deforestation, soil exhaustion, water pollution).

This process is further intensified by the multi-layered pressures to integrate national economies into the global marketplace by organizing them around the uncontrolled exploitation of resources, whether it is Zambian copper or Indonesian cocoa. Highly indebted countries desperate to earn foreign exchange are not likely to listen to lectures on sound ecological practice. The last few decades have also witnessed the transfer of low-wage dirty industries to 'free trade zones' in places like Mexico and Central America, Indonesia or the Philippines. Such investment decisions are made for a number of reasons, one being to avoid diligent enforcement of environmental regulation.

Not only do these pressures of globalization and the inequalities they generate increase environmental degradation but they also significantly narrow democratic possibilities. There has been much preaching to the Majority World about values such as 'openness', 'good governance' and 'democracy'. In World Bank documents or in the speeches of the political worthies of the West, the case for what amounts to the strong market/weak democracy model has been made ad infinitum. The problem is that, even more than in the industrial world, the economic inequalities generated by such a system are best managed by autocratic means. Political responses to these inequalities – food riots, marginalized regions seeking autonomy or independence, assertive shantytown communities or peasant organizations, trade unions wanting to break the low-wage cycle or grassroots eco-activists advocating a truly sustainable development – often have to be controlled using undemocratic and frequently heavy-handed means. Widespread crime, corruption, drugs and a 'burgeoning' underground economy further increase the tendency to use the police rather than parliament as the means of government. Majority World democracies are fragile, with a narrow basis of consensus. The strong market/weak democracy model puts too much stress on both natural environment and democratic possibilities.

Eco-democracy
In this sense the fate of the ecosystem and substantial democracy are closely linked. The defense of one increases the possibilities for the other. A decentralized, environmentally friendly approach to development could underpin a decentralized democracy where people have a real say. The political machines that compete today to protect the system – and divvy up the spoils it generates – mutilate democratic possibilities. Whatever the outcome of the various debates within the Green movement over the degree of direct democracy or decentralization, it is hard to imagine a sustainable democracy of the future that is not green.

Democracy and ecology

The mounting environmental problems – climate collapse, species endangerment, chemical poisoning, resource depletion, biogenetic hazards – can never be solved by the strong market/weak democracy model. Today climate degradation in particular has become a rallying focus for democratic movements as it becomes apparent that species survival is at stake.

As we saw in Chapter 3, CB Macpherson, in his pioneering work on the origins and nature of the strong market/weak democracy model, identifies the basis of the 'possessive individualism' that underpins the whole tradition of liberal democracy. Macpherson sees and critiques the classical tradition as being dependent on the idea of each individual maximizing their powers as a way of maximizing their desires. He identifies the 'infinite desire to possess and consume' as the source of the hoarding of power (both economic and political power) typical of market society. Writing back in the 1970s, he was optimistic that society is moving towards a post-scarcity situation where the 'compulsive labor' associated with this limitless desire will no longer be necessary.[1]

From the present viewpoint, at the end of a first decade of the 21st century characterized by triumphal but unstable capitalism, ecological crisis and persistent inequalities, this seems very optimistic. Perhaps a better starting point as a new basis for democracy is Gandhi's notion that 'there is enough for everyone's need, but not for everyone's greed'. We are facing an ecological situation where 'possessive individualism' is increasingly in conflict with species survival – including our own. Any ecological democracy would clearly need to identify and reject as its basis the classic liberal notion of the right of each individual to maximize their desires and powers. This is perhaps the most promising intersection of democratic theory with Green political thought.

1 *Democratic Theory: Essays in Retrieval*, CB Macpherson, Oxford University Press 1973.

8 Strong democracy
in the Global South

*'If you act like there is no possibility of change,
you guarantee that there will be no change.'*
Noam Chomsky, political theorist.

**In the Global South, democratic rights are often a life-
and-death question. But they are also notoriously
fragile in a situation of huge inequalities, where the
powerful frequently resort to brutal suppression to
maintain and expand their privileges. This chapter
looks at the struggle to build a more robust democracy and how it takes quite different forms based
on differing national experiences. It also examines
how such efforts can be side-tracked unless they are
deeply embedded in popular life.**

DEMOCRACY IN THE South is not yet the kind
of glitzy competition between two well-oiled media
machines you see in Washington or London. It is
something a good deal more modest but also some-
how more profound. For the Indian peasants of
Andean Latin America it may simply mean that the
military no longer comes to uproot their communities
and livelihoods and stick them in 'strategic hamlets'
for reasons of national security. In all too many places
in the Majority World it may also mean freedom from
deadly raids of ethnic militias or right-wing vigilantes
– or from getting caught in the crossfire of a dozen
civil wars. For a West African civil servant, it may
mean a modicum of security when a change of political
bosses brings in a new order. For environmentalists in
Indonesia or Malaysia, it may mean the right to the
'political space' necessary to put forward their case
about despoiling timber resources or the polluting
effects of slash-and-burn plantation practices. For an

Iranian journalist, it may mean the right simply to do their job in an honest fashion, free from the heavy hand of self-censorship. It is often experienced as a kind of negative freedom 'from' interference, a desire to secure both personal and political space.

Freedom from, freedom to

But this 'freedom from' is inevitably connected to a 'freedom to'. For there can be little dependable 'freedom from' if there is no way in which popular power can check the activities of the authorities. In the long term this can only be guaranteed if the institutions of a grassroots democracy can shape the context in which public decisions are made. Political space depends on a lively civil society and a sense on the part of the powerful that political power is not their 'private possession' to wield as they see fit. Only a strong democracy can guarantee this. Governance powers need to pass from the central authority of the national state to the rural villages, urban communities and a variety of workplaces. Such a system of dispersed power is the only way to have a chance of giving voice to the interests and ideas of the South's poor majority.

It is here, perhaps most of all, that the tradition of a strong democracy is needed to bolster popular aspirations. Already these muffled voices can be heard, although they have little impact on decision-making at the peak of the national state. The bureaucratic layers of procedural habit deem them illegitimate, even subversive. But there is no denying their existence – in the fishing villages of south India, among the dissatisfied *maquila* (sweatshop) workers along the Mexican/US border, in the native communities of Sarawak, or even amongst the shell-shocked refugees who have fled the deadly civil war in southern Sudan. They push up like stubborn crabgrass through the cracks in a cement sidewalk. They are the future seeds of a strong democracy: one that is responsive to the needs of poor people rather than to the dictates of corporate power. This is what makes them subversive.

Exporting democracy

As mentioned in Chapter 2, the Global South has in recent years (since the Cold War) been subjected to an almost constant hectoring on its undemocratic practices. Everyone from the Socialist International to the International Monetary Fund has joined the chorus. Slogans like 'good governance' and 'transparency' have become the flavor-of-the-month for the Northern advice-preaching industry. There has been a significant shift away from dictatorship and military rule to various forms of civilian rule and more-or-less freely contested elections – particularly in Latin America.

Yet democratic gains remain very fragile. There are many factors that account for this. But one of underlying significance is certainly the appropriateness of the strong market/weak democracy model in conditions of extreme poverty and inequality. This model has been virtually forced onto the nation-states of the Majority World as part of a set of conditions (for credit, access to markets, favorable trade status) demanded for participation in the global economy. It is a model in which the voice of the poor majority must be restricted to the margins of political life – for if it were at the center it would threaten to overthrow the 'market logic' that is integral to this timid brand of democracy.

The instability that inevitably flows from market-generated extremes of wealth and poverty is further aggravated by various combinations of regional, ethnic or religious tensions. The headlines may speak of hostage-taking in the southern Philippines or the deadly civil war in Sri Lanka, but the underlying story is one of racism, resentment and regional disparity. When causes are rooted in layers of historical complexity, solutions cannot be found in simply letting the market decide. Any democratic theory worth its salt would have it that people should be doing the deciding – not just as consumers but as citizens.

In Africa, meanwhile, the whole idea of the nation-state (the supposed site of democratic decision-making) has from the start been an uncomfortable fit, arbitrarily imposed as part of colonial history. Grouping peoples who had little in common and playing them off against each other was a part of colonial policy that Africans are still paying for. The postcolonial state as it evolved

---

Strong democracy: set in stone

A stone sits at the entrance to the fishing village of Kanyakumari in the south Indian state of Tamil Nadu. It is dated 20-8-1993. It literally sets in stone a victory won by the fishworkers' union against the local trawler owners. Among other things, it sets out that the trawlers are not allowed to operate during the monsoon season when fish spawn, that they must at other times return to harbor by 6pm and not fish inside a five-kilometer zone from the shore which is where the artisanal fishers (the vast majority) operate.

This local law was the fruit of a hard-fought struggle between inshore fishers and trawler owners that involved such direct actions as boat captures, road blockades and hunger strikes. For the men and the increasingly active women of Kanyakumari this law carries more weight than almost anything enacted in the faraway capital of New Delhi. As one of the militant women of Kanyakumari told the provincial fisheries minister in Madras 'Our *kal vettu* (stone inscription) is the law in our village. We can't change it. If you change it, your law will remain in your office, it can't be implemented in our village.'

This was local democratic understanding at its purest. So when the trawler-owners started to break the law – fishing in spawning season, refusing to pay for damaging the nets of inshore fishers and staying out far beyond the 6 pm limit, the community leapt into action in defense of local democracy. They marched on the local regional headquarters to demonstrate against the Collector – the highest local official, widely thought to be in the pocket of the wealthy trawler-owners. The village itself became a 'no-go' area for police (they believed the threat that they would be tossed into the ocean) and actions were taken against the trawler-owners and their employees. The community had the support of the local church and branches of national fishers' organizations. Apurna Sundar reports that, while many issues remain unresolved, 'the was both too top-heavy and lacked the capacity and often the will to service its citizens. Too often the state became a means by which the already rich and powerful extracted the wealth of society for themselves. With weak infrastructure and programs, national institutions in Africa are generally not strong – except the military, which has a long and bloody history of shaping politics to meet its own ends. But the new democratic reform agenda advocated for the South by Northern experts ignores the realities of states that lack both capacity and confidence. The demand for a withdrawal by

---

villagers did not experience the fight against trawling as a failure but as a source of empowerment. Objectively, too, it may be seen as having contributed to the building of countervailing power, the living collective consciousness of the people, their vigilance against the abuse of formal power.'

The struggle in Kanyakumari needs to be seen also as part of the overall battle that India's eight million fishworkers have successfully fought against the carve-up of Indian waters and the licensing of foreign deep-sea fishing fleets. The fishworkers' movement, spearheaded by the National Fishermen's Forum, launched a national campaign against the globalization of India's fishery. Faced with shrinking catches and with no obvious economic benefits or jobs for ordinary Indians, the organizers saw little choice. They used the same direct-action tactics as the people of Kanyakumari, launching a series of national fishery strikes, blockades of major harbors and hunger strikes. They also drew on the organization of fishers in hundreds of small seaside communities like Kanyakumari to co-ordinate action locally and spread the word.

Another parallel between these national and local democratic struggles is the ideology of a kind of eco-democracy which emerged from both struggles. In both cases, the themes of the protest were social injustice (the privilege of the few at the expense of the many), the unsustainable pillaging of fish stocks by mechanical means and the potent argument that the food security of Indians should come before the needs of the export market. Both protests used the spaces provided by liberal democracy to expand the 'political space' for a stronger popular grassroots democracy. ∎

Information drawn from Aparna Sundar, 'Sea changes: organizing around the fishery in a South Indian community', in Jonathan Barker, *Street-level Democracy*, Between the Lines, Toronto 1999.

the state from both regulatory functions and basic economic protections for the marginalized will never inspire popular confidence. So the limits on democracy intrinsic to the strong market/weak democracy model simply aggravate tensions and inequalities that already afflict Majority World society.

Revival of interest

There is a tradition of struggle for a stronger democracy in the South. Elements of it can be seen in parts of the Pan-Africanist movement and in Julius Nyerere's attempts to craft an African socialism for Tanzania; in the radical tradition of Bolivar, Sandino and Zapata in Latin American populism that has acted as an inspiration for both the Sandinistas of Nicaragua and the Zapatistas of southern Mexico; and in currents of Gandhian direct action in South Asia. Such strong democracy traditions were smothered during the Cold War contest between market democracy (and the military dictatorships often used to preserve it) and the various forms of autocratic state socialism supported by the Soviet Union. By and large, these socialisms, as witnessed in places like Mengistu's Ethiopia or Pol Pot's Kampuchea (Cambodia), totally lacked any type of democratic credentials. They turned into human-rights nightmares and killing grounds. Other countries such as China, Vietnam and Cuba could at least boast of some achievements in meeting people's basic needs. They are, however, hardly models of strong democracy. So for a whole period of post-colonial history innovation with popular forms of democracy was simply pushed off the agenda.

There is now a revival of interest in the traditions of a strong democracy. Today, these blend with radical notions of indigenous self-determination, community and regional empowerment, ecological resistance, a strong civil society and economic democracy to form the fragments of an alternative to the strong market/ weak democracy model. These ideas are drawing a citizenry who feel disenfranchised (whether they are allowed to cast a ballot or not) from a form of government where the tune is called in Washington or Brussels or where foreign interests work in concert with the domestic powerholders who benefit most from the globalization of the economic life. A desire for a 'strong democracy' is inspired by a growing revulsion over the gross disparities in 'life chances' between those in the walled luxury compounds of Guatemala City or Nairobi and those clinging to existence in the urban shantytowns and marginalized villages that dot the South.

The movement to deepen democracy inevitably looks very different from one country to another. Looking at another country as a model is a bad idea. In some, as in Bolivia, it takes the form of a new constitution (introduced by the Government of Evo Morales) empowering a poor indigenous majority. In Burma it means a movement for change led by activist Buddhist monks. In Iran and China it involves the use of the internet and the blogosphere to circumvent state censorship. Differences in activist resources, in the level of development, political traditions, and the undemocratic enemies to be faced will all shape both the struggle and the results. This is why exporting US-style democracy to the rest of the world is not just self-serving but futile. In the US itself, any deepening of democracy will have to reshape the dominant forms of individualism in US culture to recreate a citizenship that is likely to entail a much higher level of individual autonomy than one is ever likely to see in the more collective societies of the South.

Struggles for a stronger democracy in India or Nigeria will have to draw on sources of strength (collective identities, indigenous forms of organization) that are rooted in those places.

Strong democracy in the Global South

Creating democratic space

A prerequisite for any kind of strong democracy is the popular belief that it is both desirable and possible. One source of these convictions is people's experience in running their own organizations and practicing democracy on a local level. Whether it is cocoa-producer co-ops like Kuapa Kokoo in Ghana, or shantytown dwellers' associations struggling to improve living conditions in Lima and Mexico City – democratic experience helps create a confidence and belief in self-rule. Throughout the South such practices of local democracy are emerging in a variety of settings. Some have been inspired and supported by Northern non-governmental organizations (NGOs). Others have grown out of people's collective attempts to secure their economic security – co-ops of craft workers or of farmers and fishers, vendors' associations which democratically set the rules for trade in urban markets. Some organizations have grown up to protect workers' rights, such as trade unions or other worker advocate groups. Others spring from churches, mosques or temples where they advocate the welfare of their members and often the broader community. Some are influenced by the ideas of feminism and form associations to fight for gender rights, against domestic violence, or to create income-generating schemes for their members – a brave example here is the Afghan organization Women for Women. Democratic groups have also formed to fight for minority or regional rights. Lower-caste groups in India and gay and lesbian rights organizations everywhere it is possible for them to organize are just two of many such struggles.

A kind of grassroots environmentalism has also grown up in many countries to defend the resources of 'the commons' – water, land, trees, fishing rights, watersheds, air quality – against attempts to privatize, pollute or otherwise expropriate them from public use. This is a particularly important struggle for indigenous peoples who still depend on the resources of the commons as part of 'a survival economy'. Still other kinds of organization grow out of the margins of desperation. Refugees try to exercise some minimal control over their lives in the encampments that dot Africa and parts of Asia. Street vendors fight against harassment by the police.

The sites and motivations for this kind of local democracy vary widely. But we can find here the flesh and blood of a potential strong democracy. For without the self-confidence and personal experience of democratic practice, demands for popular control are made in a vacuum. Without the sense that self-rule is possible, 'democracy' will be simply more rhetoric from the political class. Without a democratic ethos to infuse political culture, 'democracy' will remain an exotic foreign import from the West unlikely to flower in conditions of desperate poverty and repressive inequality. Such an 'imported democracy' will always be tainted by its association with big power bullying and corporate maneuvering to obtain access to natural resources, exemptions from environmental or labor standards and extensive tax holidays. Only practices of democracy that are part of daily life will prevent it from becoming another ossified hypocrisy used by those with power to trick those below them.

Brutal resistance

The struggles to create the local political space for democracy have, however, proved long and difficult. Resistance from above has been fierce and many activists have paid with their lives, from Haiti to East Timor. The brutality of the Indonesian military and its associated militias in East Timor up to the country's independence in 2002 stands as a kind of template for the brutality with which undemocratic power and privilege is defended in the South. Tens of thousands have died over decades in a struggle to create a self-determined democracy beyond the reach of the mandarins in Jakarta. Yet, as is so often the case, the heroism of activists in the streets and mountains was not enough. It took a combination of the political collapse of the corrupt Suharto dictatorship, severe economic crisis, exceptional international pressure and solidarity to force the Indonesian military first to allow a referendum and then eventually to withdraw from East Timor. The democracy movement in Burma faces similar circumstances today. A democratic impulse from below usually needs either some encouragement from above or else an exceptional set of 'crisis circumstances' that open a space of democratic possibility. It is in such conditions that there is the chance of building the institutions of popular power that would guarantee a strong democracy.

Institutionalizing strong democracy

One place where strong democracy has gained a foothold is the southern Brazilian city of Porto Alegre. Here, under the inspiration of the *Partido dos Trabalhadores* (Brazilian Workers' Party) the municipal government is organized around a high level of popular participation. As in many Brazilian cities, the municipal budget was subject to the corrupting influence of a traditional patronage machine. A study of local finances in parts of Brazil indicates that as much as 64 per cent of the total budget was misappropriated in this way.

In 1988 the Partido dos Trabalhadores initiated a process of popular review of Porto Alegre's budget, involving local community meetings at which priorities are set and then further meetings when they are voted on. In the 1996 budget some 100,000 of Porto Alegre's citizens participated in this budgetary process. Even though the Workers' Party has lost power in Porto Alegre, the new mayor José Fogaça has continued the experiment in participatory budgeting – a testimony to the program's popularity. There are now about 70 cities in Brazil and the rest of Latin America that are trying to develop their own versions of participatory budgeting and planning based on the inspiration of Porto Alegre.

A similar level of strong participation can be seen in the *Panchayat* (village assembly) empowerment movement in the rural villages of West Bengal. In addition to one of the most radical land reform movements in India, the Left Front Government there instituted a level of Panchayat reform in order 'to increase the opportunities for members of disadvantaged classes (including women and untouchables) to wield public power'. The process included opportunity for budget review and significant local planning powers.[1] In 2007 Panchayat power rebounded against the Left Front Government over its violent seizure of peasant land to set up a free trade zone. Tricky business, this democracy.

In the subcontinent's southwestern state of Kerala, under the leadership of the Communist Party of India, a series of 'development seminars' with around 300,000 participants in 1997-98 taught villagers basic self-governance skills. Ambitious plans called for some 40 per cent of the state budget to be taken from powerful departments in the bureaucracy and devolved to about 900 individual Panchayat village planning councils. The result has been thoughtful plans with high levels of popular participation in at least some of the villages and an enriching of the democratic process throughout the region with 'the creation of grassroots neighborhood-level groups in hundreds of villages'. Kerala has set aside 19 February as a special day to celebrate the benefits of Panchayat self-governance.

Strong democracy in the Global South

In Venezuela, the controversial government of Hugo Chávez has encouraged community councils to take over some of the functions of municipal governments and the national state. Thousands of such councils have formed across the country – with mixed results but high levels of participation – particularly in poor barrios. The jury is still out as to whether this experiment in direct democracy will extend an anti-bureaucratic people's power or be manipulated and smothered from above. But democratic sentiment remains strong in the country, with a 2007 continent-wide poll by the Chilean firm Latinobarometro showing only Uruguayans having more confidence in their democratic institutions.[2] A recent study by the Chilean political scientist David Altman celebrates Uruguay as the country most hospitable to direct democracy through referenda and popular input into constitutional change in the Western Hemisphere (see box).

It seems people like to have a say.

Uruguay: home of direct democracy

Uruguay is known as the 'Switzerland of Latin America', mostly because of its small size and traditional peaceful political stability. It is the oldest unbroken democracy in Latin America – with the notable exception of the period of US-backed military dictatorship (1973-85) that aimed to forestall demands for radical change.

What is less well known is the similarity between Uruguay and Switzerland when it comes to giving their citizens a direct say in important political matters. Since 1917 there have been 37 national referenda and plebiscites in Uruguay over such important matters as constitutional reform (both yea and nay), an amnesty for the military (nay), protection of pensions (yea), partial withdrawal of Privatization Law (yea), and inclusion of water as a basic human right in the constitution (yea).

Direct democracy initiatives can be triggered from below by gathering signatures, and unpopular laws can be challenged in a similar fashion. Continent-wide poll findings in 2007 indicate that Uruguayans hold their democratic institutions in higher regard than do any other people in South America. ∎

David Altman, Research Centre on Direct Democracy, Geneva.

Beyond capturing power

Both the Brazilian and the Indian examples show a tendency towards designing a process of 'people's planning' from below. In both cases these moves can be seen as part of a process whereby traditional centralized (indeed Leninist) Left political parties are reorienting themselves to create organs of decentralized popular political power outside party control. The West Bengal case indicates the difficulties inherent in doing this. These are both situations where significant democratic impulses from below 'were given life and successfully scaled up and were underwritten by a political project and given state support' – although by state here we are, significantly, talking about regional and municipal (rather than national) political power. In these cases the parties involved have shifted their ideals from seizing or taking over power to dispersing it in a decentralized, democratic fashion.

This contrasts with a number of other situations in the South, quite visible in South Africa, Iran and the Philippines, where powerful and often sophisticated movements helped create social transformations. In all such cases the governments brought to power at least partially through the agency of social movements have then sought to 'normalize' situations and undercut the power of the movements, curtailing their ambitions for a strong democracy. While all these situations are still in flux, a pattern clearly emerges of governments either with their own agenda (clerical conservatism in the case of Iran) or subject to the pressures of a neoliberal global consensus. This neoliberal agenda (as enforced by the IMF and the US State Department) is often adopted as the only course of action or at least the course of least resistance. In such situations the governments quickly move to monopolize power, rather than to disperse it, so as to impose unpopular measures.

The African National Congress (ANC) Government in post-apartheid South Africa, for example, rules with the good will and overwhelming support of the black population. It has, however, sought to exercise a technocratic control of the process of decentralization and grassroots empowerment that still exists in its various program documents. This is now being challenged by the Zuma faction of the ANC, which is making claims to return the party to its social-movement roots.

Sociologist Patrick Heller notes that: 'Although the ANC was brought to power by a broad-based popular liberation movement, it has consolidated its power through the negotiation phase as the singular representative of the liberation struggle and subsequently through its control of the state. As the electorally mandated agent of national democratic transformation, and as a party in power, the ANC has squarely rejected mobilization and protest politics as instruments of democratic deepening and development. It has accordingly acted to co-opt or distance itself from its social movement partners, or to transform them into service delivery agents.'[3]

This is a sad judgment on what many throughout Africa had hoped would be an exemplary process of democratization that would shake up the continent's political culture. But it fits with what has happened in many other parts of the Global South. When power is 'captured' and treated as something to be guarded and protected – rather than extended and dispersed – then democratic possibilities are stunted.

Nationalism replaces democracy

In the Horn of Africa both the Eritrean and Ethiopian liberation movements fought for decades against the brutal authoritarianism of General Mengistu's regime in Addis Ababa. Those who barely escaped the General's 'Red Terror' campaign fled to the mountains and deserts where they slowly built an armed opposition. Their implicit (and sometimes explicit) promise was of a different way of doing politics. Anyone who witnessed the heroism and sacrifice of those years of struggle could not but believe this promise. Years spent living in caves and building schools and factories hidden from marauding MiG fighter jets under the meager cover of the region's vegetation, gave their cause an heroic cast of almost epic proportions.

Yet when these struggles finally bore fruit in a military victory, democracy was slow to come. Power became a 'thing' to be defended rather than a process to be extended and cultivated. As so often in the conditions of fragile nationhood in the post-colonial South, the ideology of the 'nation besieged' replaced a commitment to popular democracy as the glue to hold things together. It was only a matter of years before the two 'liberation governments' in Addis and Asmara were dispatching troops to their common border to renew the slaughter. This time round, the cause was much less noble (a few hundred meters of rocky ground plus increasingly obscure national grievances). The euphoria of liberation victory gave way to fear and despair. On both sides the goodwill and hopes of some of the poorest people on the globe were squandered on the altar of nationalism.

One cannot help but speculate what would have happened if the 'post-liberation' period had been devoted to the difficult but ultimately more promising task of extending power to the villages, regions and workplaces of the Horn, as, for example, President Thomas Sankara tried to do in Burkina Faso before he was assassinated. While this would have been a challenge in a regional situation fraught with tension and distrust, it would at least have been a goal worthy of the hopes rooted in the sacrifice made by so many. Instead we had the familiar rhetoric of 'consolidating the revolution'. It is a situation that has echoes from Hanoi to Havana. As so often in the past, this meant the established leaderships in both Addis and Asmara clinging to power at all costs. In such situations opposition and even constructive criticism are seen to verge on treason. The liberation struggle gets narrowed to the power of a leadership progressively divorced from those who had fought so hard for something different. Without the broader goals and trust necessary for a popular democracy, nationalism becomes the only glue. Sometimes the results are merely an ossification and limitation of a still heroic revolution – as can be seen with Cuba's ageing Castro brothers clinging to power in defiance of Washington. Other times, as in the Horn, it can lead to a slaughter of the innocents.

High-stakes poker

So the stakes are high for building a strong democracy in the Global South. The likelihood of equitable and sustainable development without the institutions of a popular democracy is almost non-existent. An economic policy based on opening up Southern domestic economies to corporate-led globalization will only increase the inequality and environmental devastation. While some may prosper, most will have their lives uprooted and end up with little to show for it. Their per-capita income may increase as they are forced into the margins of the cash economy, but without unions and political organizations to represent them they will remain there. Popular power is needed to shape a society where the wealthy pay adequate taxes, where environmental and labor standards are respected and where collective goods (such as water, housing, cheap public transportation, safe communities and good air) are guaranteed. This will not happen without those who benefit most by it having an effective voice in making sure it does.

Without this kind of strong democracy the South will continue to be plagued by autocratic tendencies generated at least in part by discontents with the corruption and double-dealing of the strong market/

weak democracy model. If democracy is simply the excuse for one gang stealing the goodies, other gangs are likely to rebel against it. Democratic alignments then form around regions or groups that feel they simply have been left out and that it is now 'their turn'. Significant policy differences are not part of such a political culture. If a new gang gets in, nothing changes but how the goodies are distributed and to whom. Such a situation also generates pressure to overthrow corrupt (if elected) politicians. Witness the military uprisings that plagued Latin America in the 1970s and continue to plague parts of Asia and much of Africa today.

More recently, the popular reaction to democratic pilfering has been religious fundamentalism. This may be Islamic in the Middle East, Africa and Asia, Hindu in India or Christian in Latin America. Such ideologies feed on the corruption and scandal associated with the politics of market democracy. They pit their higher spiritual values against the corrupt materialism associated with 'Marx and Coca-Cola'. The sad choice between fundamentalism and market democracy is well caught in the title of Benjamin Barber's excellent book *Jihad vs McWorld*.[4] The outrages of 9/11 and the subsequent polarizations associated with the 'war on terror' have devalued democracy through the use of torture, 'shock-and-awe militarism', and the creeping blueprint of a global international security state.

Fundamentalists have become more powerful in response to crude US bullying. The reforming zeal of actual fundamentalist regimes varies greatly, although it almost never includes commitments to extending power beyond a narrow ruling circle who can correctly interpret the scripture of policy.

There is a built-in instability in both the politics and economics of market democracy. Boom-and-bust business cycles. Grab-it-while-you-can politicians.

Corporations always ready to move on to greener (fewer taxes, cheaper workers) pastures. The politics of resentment. Democratic rhetoric used to cloak naked self-interest. The volatile speculation of global financial transactions. The bursting financial bubbles of the 2008/09 economic meltdown make this difficult to deny for even the most ardent market enthusiasts.

It is understandable, yet odd, that conventional political science is obsessed with 'political stability' while it champions the very forces that undermine it. The long-term consequences of these instabilities are too often war and civil war, food shortages and famine, the mass movement of refugees, bankruptcy and the cutting back of essential services. The same forces are at work in the industrial North, although the impacts there are more buffered. A strong democracy, while not guaranteeing stability, would certainly increase the chances. Large sections of the population would, if they had a real democratic stake in the system, be less likely to be swayed by demagogues and the politics of resentment. They would be more likely to defend democratic gains if these were threatened. Strong democracy would enhance the chances for both healthy (as opposed to repressive) political stability and an equitable and sustainable form of development. People would have a chance to insist upon it.

1 Achon Fung and Erik Olin Wright, 'Deepening Democracy: Innovation in Empowered Participatory Governance', *Politics and Society*, 2001. **2** 'Venezuela lets councils bloom', Juan Forero, *Washington Post*, 17 May 2007. **3** Patrick Heller, 'Moving the State: The Politics of Democratic Decentralization in Kerala, South Africa and Porto Alegre', *Politics and Society*, March 2001. **4** Benjamin Barber, *Jihad vs McWorld*, Random House, New York 1996.

8 Conclusion

'The job of a citizen is to keep his/her mouth open.'
Noam Chomsky, political theorist.

Democracy involves risk. This is what is most difficult for many of its advocates to accept, even those who see themselves as risk-takers when it comes to entrepreneurial matters. And democracy is always messy: lots of meetings and reversed decisions. But we owe it to ourselves and the peace of the world to get involved and take on the responsibilities that real democracy puts on us.

WHILE EVERYONE IS in favor of democracy in principle, they want some guarantee that the outcomes will be something they approve of. This is ultimately the logic behind the 'weak democracy/strong market' model. If you take a number of matters out of the hands of democratic decision-makers and instead make them the sole preserve of the market you can limit the impact of unpredictable democracy. If the market is more important than democracy, there will be no confiscatory wealth taxes, no increases in the minimum wage, no controls on capital, no unwelcome competition from the public sector. If you already have money and power this will safeguard you from an 'excess' of democracy that overflows its riverbanks and might wash away some of your property. If you hit economic turbulence you can count on the government to help you out because everything depends on the health of the market and you are 'too big to fail'. But what if those who dominate the strong market behave irresponsibly and endanger the economic well-being of the rest of us (as we saw recently in the credit crunch with the derivatives market/sub-prime mortgage scandal)? Should we not have the democratic clout to keep them in check?

Conclusion

But it is not just the self-interested wealthy that worry about the risks of democracy. Many enlightened people are concerned that expanding its scope will lead to an offensive of populist reaction. They fear a generalized assault along a number of fronts: reinstituting capital punishment, outlawing abortion, an attack on gay rights, an end to foreign aid, or defunding social programs through radical tax cuts. These are real fears. But are they enough to place limits on democracy?

It is inevitable that, in a strong democracy, more issues will become politicized than is currently the case. Under the present model of neoliberal consensus, a great number of what should be debatable public issues have been depoliticized. Whether in the fields of urban planning or of the approval of new pharmaceuticals or agrochemicals, it is assumed to be simply a question of the judgment of disinterested experts.

A more politicized environment with greater citizen capacity to initiate legislation would allow advocates of capital punishment to try to push their case. This is an issue that would need to be battled out. Similarly, introducing more proportionality into the electoral system would allow not only more representation from a principled Left and ecological parties but potentially could allow fascist members of parliament, as it does in several European countries. It is hard to see how such risks can be avoided if we want a more profound democracy.

One possibility explored by the French political theorist Chantel Mouffe in her book, *The Democratic Paradox*, is a balance between the strong democracy tradition and that of individual rights rooted more in the liberal version of weak democracy. According to this prescription, certain rights – say basic civil rights, a woman's right to choose, freedom from discrimination, a sanctity of the person which would preclude capital punishment – would be placed (via a bill of rights enforced by an independent judiciary) beyond the reach of popular decision-making. This would, however, provide a clear opening for those who would want to place their property rights in the same category. Also, with the political role involved in selecting judges, an independent judiciary cannot be guaranteed. This was made blatantly apparent by the intervention of the US Republican-dominated Supreme Court in resolving the Florida 2000 results of the Bush-Gore presidential election in favor of the Republican candidate.

So even if the tradition of strong democracy is qualified by some kind of charter or constitutional guarantee of individual rights, this would hardly stop a debate over what rights should and should not be covered. The risk may be modified but it is not removed.

Similarly, a commitment to decentralized decision-making would have to allow local communities and neighborhoods to make decisions that might well fly in the face of accepted norms. This will sometimes result in outcomes that many might regard as negative. Say a community decides under the influence of a powerful real estate lobby to tear down a marvelous old historical building and put up luxury condos. Conservation activists might battle against such a project but in the end wouldn't they have to accept the results?

There are several caveats that should be added here. One is that it is far more likely that local people would appreciate the value of an historical building or an unpolluted stream that they pass by every day and would want to preserve them. On the other hand, a remote industrial zoning board staffed by bureaucrats and political appointees would probably not share that appreciation. Another is that under conditions of a strong democracy where communities get to vote directly on issues it would be necessary to ensure a level playing field. In the case of the fight over whether or not to keep a heritage building, strict spending limits would have to be observed so that powerful interests could not simply 'buy' the results they desired. Access to media would also have to be equalized. A third caveat is that there are some issues of such profound moral weight – say the use of torture by the police or a popularly sanctioned campaign of ethnic cleansing against a vilified minority – where even a democratically taken decision would have to be actively resisted.

Another point to keep in mind is that democracy is always messy. Meetings go on far too long. People disagree and march in the streets; sometimes they even throw stones. Everything is questioned. All decisions seem provisional. They may be reopened next week or next decade. People are recalcitrant and stubborn. Things move much more slowly than many feel they should. And then there is all that constant questioning. It is this that offends our managerial sense of things. It is also true that some will inevitably be more active than others. This however will be mitigated by the latent possibility of a more passive majority deciding to intervene once they feel the pendulum has swung too far in a particular direction. In conditions of more localized and direct democracy this will always be an option.

We should be wary of simply applying the mechanisms of a strong democracy to contemporary situations and prejudices. As Marx warned, there is a danger in trying to compose the 'music of the future' in today's circumstances. A society with a high level of self-rule would be built on a citizenship and political knowledge and engagement quite different from that shown by today's passive and often resentful voter. It would occur in a situation of not just more democratic political mechanisms but one where the whole economy and culture is infused with democratic values and practices. This is not to say that all short-sighted decisions and selfishness would be banished (if only!) but simply that they would be more easily *identified* as such, rather than being treated as the common sense of an ethos based on self-interest and might-makes-right.

An ethos of citizenship to replace or at least subordinate passive political consumerism is the only real hope for reviving democracy. The petty resentments and cynicism about all public life spawned by the notion that all politicians (like all brands of cola) are ultimately the same is a dead end. We need a citizenry that goes beyond blaming politicians and 'throwing the rascals out' to one that takes responsibility for the direction of society. A strong democracy depends on greater equality and on this notion of active citizenship and engagement. This is the very thing that the political class and the journalists, spin-doctors, and opinion-managers who serve it find messy and threatening.

There is an excitement involved with people feeling their own power and gaining confidence in their own capacities for self-rule. Anyone with experience in people running their own housing or food co-op has felt some of this contagious enthusiasm. The possibilities for a generalized self-management have some chance of shifting popular interest from compensatory needs (passive entertainments, consumerism, workaholism, various addictions) to participation in an enriched and empowered public realm. This will, of course, be a question of degree. But the experience in situations like Barcelona in the 1930s, the Paris Commune of 1871, Hungary in 1956, or the civic engagement in the immediate post-colonial period throughout much of the South gives some grounds for optimism. The altruism brought out by these brief experiences gives some sense of the potential for empowerment in conditions of strong democracy.

A perfect democracy is of course an impossibility. Democracy is, in a sense, a constant horizon we must strive to reach. Undemocratic concentrations of power will always form and need dissolving. Cliques and cabals will need challenging. Civil-service empires will need to be deconstructed. Democracy will never stand still: if it is not expanding, it is very likely contracting. As the famous British historian EH Carr pointed out: 'To speak today of the defense of democracy as if we were defending something which we knew and had possessed for many decades or centuries is self-deception... we should be nearer the mark, and should have a more convincing slogan, if we spoke of the need not to defend democracy, but to create it.'

But how to 'create' democracy? A key to achieving a stronger democracy is a different attitude towards power. There needs to evolve a pole on the political spectrum around the notion that power isn't just a 'thing' to be captured and wielded for particular policy ends. A different attitude would see power as something that needs to be dispersed and embedded in everything from workplaces to self-governing communities. While it would still exist at national and international levels, these would no longer be automatically 'superior' to local levels of popular power; rather they would coexist in a complex set of negotiations and checks-and-balances.

A more equal economy with democracy built into the workplace is crucial to this effort. The economy today exerts a constant pull that is used to 'discipline' democracy with what is 'realistic'; to keep some in poverty and others in villas, BMWs and stock options. But even if the essential element of democracy is built into the economy, accumulations of privilege will continue to be an anti-democratic irritant. We'll need to replace our passive consumerist democracy with a reinvigorated polity to provide us with a platform to fight for fairness and equal rights against the blinkered technocrats and free-market globalizers. The inequality generated by the strong market/weak democracy model undermines the mutuality and solidarity between people in society. This inevitably leads to a politics of polarization and resentment between classes, genders, regions and ethnic groups. As we saw in Chapter 8, this is particularly true of the cleavages that are ripping apart political entities across the poor Majority World. To build a strong democracy based on a 'popular sovereignty' that is more than a convenient fiction is the potential beginning of sanity, stability and sustainability. We all know by now what more politics-as-usual will mean.

It may be that democracy will always be unfinished business. But it is *our* business. Let's take it back.

CONTACTS

Australia

Centre for Deliberative Democracy & Global Governance
deliberativedemocracy.anu.edu.au
Advocates for an international approach based on deliberative democracy.

Women Into Politics
www.womenintopolitics.org.au
Has produced a Women's Charter for political reform.

Britain

Building Global Democracy Programme
Centre for the Study of Globalization and Regionalization, University of Warwick.
info@buildingglobaldemocracy.org
An organization that promotes extending democracy into the international sphere.

Unlock Democracy
www.unlockdemocracy.org.uk
Incorporates the Charter 88 Movement and campaigns for deepening democracy on a number of fronts.

Canada

Democracy Watch
www.dwatch.ca
Aims to clean up governments and corporations and make them more popularly accountable.

Fair Vote Canada
www.fairvotecanada.org
A movement pushing for reform, greater proportionality and fairness in the Canadian electoral system.

Rights and Democracy
www.dd-rd.ca
Advocates for democracy in the Global South.

United States

FairVote
www.fairvote.org
Acts to transform US elections to gain universal access to participation.

Small Planet Institute
www.smallplanet.org
Aims to further a worldwide shift towards democracy.

International

Connexions Online
www.connexions.org
Resources and contacts about workers' self-management.

DD Meeting Place
democracy.mkolar.org
Offers a host of international direct democracy weblinks.

Democratic Audit
www.democraticaudit.com
An organization providing the tools for measuring democratic integrity and effectiveness worldwide.

E-Democracy.Org
forums.e-democracy.org
Online town hall network of local issues across Britain, New Zealand/Aotearoa and the US.

Economic Democracy for the Americas
www.ecodema.org
Promotes economic democracy.

International Institute for Democracy and Electoral Assistance (IDEA)
www.idea.int
An intergovernmental agency that supports sustainable democracy worldwide. Based in Stockholm, it has regional offices in Africa, Asia and Latin America and at the UN.

Movement for Direct Democracy
movementfordirectdemocracy.com
Produces a periodic newsletter on
direct democracy issues.

Third World Network
www.twnside.org
Coalition of Southern NGOs with an
action, research, publishing focus.

Combines powerful analysis with
effective international lobbying.

**World Forum for Democratization
in Asia**
www.wfda.net
Holds conferences on how to deepen
Asian democracy.

Bibliography

Books

Anthony Arblaster, *Democracy*,
University of Minnesota Press,
Minneapolis, 1987.

Jonathan Barker (ed), *Street-Level
Democracy*, Between The Lines,
Toronto, 1999.

Ian Budge, *The New Challenge of
Direct Democracy*, Polity Press,
Cambridge, 1996.

C Douglas Lummis, *Radical
Democracy*, Cornell University Press,
Ithaca, 1996.

Joan Menieri and Paul Getsos, *Tools
for Radical Democracy*, Wiley, 2007.

Sheldon S Wolin, *Democracy Inc*,
Princeton University Press 2008.

Journals/periodicals

Review of African Political Economy
editor@roape.org
Covers the blockages both internal and
external to the evolution of popular
democracy in Africa.

Politics and Society
via www.sagepub.com/journals

Index